T-Shirts and Suits
A Guide to the Business of Creativity

David Parrish

Merseyside
acme
DEVELOPING CREATIVE INDUSTRIES

T-Shirts and Suits

Royal College of Art

Key Points

1   Some people think that creativity and business don't mix. I disagree. Think of business and creativity as partners, not opposites.

2   Combine the best ideas of both T-shirts and Suits to turn your creative talent into income streams.

3   Creative talent does not automatically 'deserve' business success. Not all creative ideas make feasible businesses.

4   Making a business out of creativity does not involve selling out – so long as you invent the right business formula.

5   As well as a creative product or service, you will need to create a unique and feasible business formula.

6   Be clear about your own definition of success. Know where you want to get to – your Vision.

7   Clarify your specific business Mission.

8   Recognise and hold on to your Values.

9   Decide whether now is the right time to start or expand.

10 These principles apply to not-for-profit organisations as well as commercial businesses.

Ideas in Action

Sharon Mutch
Photographic Artist

Sharon Mutch is an artist with a passion for her work and a head for business.

Her artistic passion is born of her experience. "During the second year of my Fine Art degree I suffered an ectopic pregnancy and nearly died. I began to incorporate this experience into my photographic art and many of my works are images of women: *Feminae in Vitro* (Women within Glass) is the name of the collection of my work," she said.

After graduation, Sharon exhibited at several high-profile photographers' galleries. "However, the timing was not right for me. I recognised immediately that my work was strong in both imagery, content and depth of meaning. I also realised that the emotive symbolism of my work hit a raw nerve with many women regardless of social status, views and personal experience. Even though my work was receiving quite a bit of attention, I felt as though I didn't belong in the 'art world', that it was happening too quickly," she recalled.

Nine years later she unwrapped the dust sheets from her work and felt the time was right to go into business and she set up as a sole trader. "I am the artist and I am also my manager / agent, my business brain is the ruling factor when it comes to commission rates, gallery representation and marketing," she explains. Her business brain decided to

approach the top art markets in the world: New York, London and Paris. She was prepared to 'say no' to lesser opportunities so as to concentrate all her efforts on breaking into New York City's Chelsea and Soho area despite being advised by the British Consulate that this is "the most difficult art scene in the world for finding gallery representation".

Sharon was aware of the challenge but she also knew that if she could succeed here, then other exhibitions and sales would follow. Having devised her strategy she researched the selected markets, at first through desk research, trawling websites and examining galleries' submissions criteria. With the help of UK Trade and Investment's 'Passport to Export' scheme, and the assistance of the British Consulate in New York, she attended the New York Art Expo and visited galleries with her portfolio. This resulted in offers of exhibitions from two galleries and she chose the Viridian Artists Gallery. Her work was exhibited there in July / August 2005.

This success – which will no doubt lead to other exhibitions and sales – was the result not only of artistic passion and talent but also of using a business head to break into the difficult yet lucrative New York market.

www.sharonmutch.com

'Vessel of Confinement' © **Sharon Mutch**

Links to related ideas and topics in book:

✱ **Combining the best of 'T-shirts' and 'Suits'** (see pg 8)
✱ **The timing of setting up in business** (see pg 12)
✱ **Targeting specific markets / customers** (see pg 36)
✱ **Market Research** (see pg 38)
✱ **Saying No** (see pg 92)

2

Know Yourself

— In this chapter we look at a technique for objectively assessing your own strengths and weaknesses as part of the process of finding your feasible business formula.
— We look at the core competencies on which you can build your creative enterprise.
— In addition there are some thoughts about learning, training and continuing professional development.

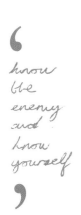

'know the enemy and know yourself'

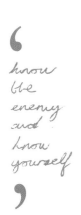
PRIMEFACT checklist

In *The Art of War*, Chinese military strategist Sun Tzu wrote: "If you know the enemy and know yourself, your victory will not stand in doubt".[8]

Whether or not you regard business as a kind of warfare,[9] his point is that knowing one's own strengths and weaknesses will help you to decide when, how and where to proceed. It will help you recognise the customers, competition and conditions that are most likely to suit you – or not. Yet 'knowing ourselves', in the sense of making objective and critical assessments of our shortcomings and special qualities, is very difficult. It is much easier to assess another enterprise than our own and that's why it is useful to get outsiders' views if we are to get a clear picture of ourselves.

Knowing yourself applies not only to your personal creativity, skills and aptitudes. We need to understand the strengths and weaknesses of our business or organisation taking into account all the people involved in the core team and wider 'family' of stakeholders including associates and advisers. We also need to assess our assets, reputation, knowledge of the market and intellectual capital.

Evaluating Strengths and Weaknesses

Rather than simply attempting to write down all the strengths and weaknesses we can think of on a blank sheet of paper, the **PRIMEFACT checklist** on the following page provides a useful structure for a comprehensive analysis.

I devised this checklist specifically for the creative and cultural industries and have used it successfully with a range of clients.

Intellectual Property
see page 54
___

Market Research
see page 38
___

Values
see page 11
___

Finances
see page 64
___

The PRIMEFACT Checklist

People
What are the strengths and weaknesses of our people?
Employees, directors, members, associates, advisers and other stakeholders.

Reputation (or Brand)
What is our reputation with our target customers? What are the strengths – or weaknesses – of our brand or brands?

Intellectual Property
What intellectual property do we have? How is it protected? How easily can it be turned into income streams?

Market Research / Market Information
What information do we have about market segments and market trends? What do we know about individual clients and their specific needs?

Ethos (or Values or Culture)
What is our ethos, our values and our organisational culture? Do all stakeholders subscribe to this same ethos?

Finances (ie Money)
What is the current state of profitability, cashflow and assets? How much money do we have to invest or can we borrow?

Agility (or Nimbleness or Change-ability)
Are we agile enough to seize new opportunities?
Are people prepared to change and ready for change?
Are there barriers to change?

Collaborators (Alliances, Partnerships and Networks)
What are the strengths and weaknesses of our associations with other businesses and organisations (including government)?

Talents (Competencies and Skills)
What are our core competencies?
What skills do we have available and what gaps are there?
How will we learn new skills?

Be frank about your weaknesses too. Remember that not all weaknesses need to be fixed. Maybe you can find a new market position where your weaknesses are not so significant. The important thing here is to recognise your strengths and weaknesses *in relation to competitors*. You may have a particular strength, but if your competitors have it too, or are even better, then it does not give you **Competitive Advantage**.

Competitive Advantage
see page 45

Core Competencies

Core Competencies

Your **Core Competencies** are the key skills on which you base your business success. These are often 'deeper' than first thought.

For example Canon recognised that their core competencies were not in cameras, but more fundamentally in optics and this allowed them to see that they could transfer their expertise into the photocopier market. Similarly Sony's core competency is not electronics but miniaturisation; Honda's is not cars but engines – which helped them see beyond cars into motor boat and lawnmower markets. Richard Branson's Virgin brand is fundamentally about customer service, so it can be applied not only to music but also to airlines, trains, financial services and mobile phones.

Some theatre companies view their core competency as 'communicating a message' using drama – rather than drama in its own right. In some cases web designers have a core competency in branding and marketing consultancy. Peppered Sprout's core competency is not publishing but 'delivering ideas to clients'.

Deep down, what are your core competencies?

Ideas in Action — see page 24

The Hedgehog

One of the reasons to assess your competitive strengths is to answer the question: What can your business be world-class at? Note that the question is not what you *would like* to be world-class at, but what you *can* be. Knowing this, and then playing ruthlessly to your key strength, is part of a successful **Hedgehog Strategy**.[10]

Hedgehog Strategy

The fox, renowned for his cunning, has many strategies for killing the hedgehog.[11] On the other hand, the hedgehog has only one strategy for defending itself. Whenever the fox attacks, from whatever direction, the hedgehog rolls itself into a ball of spikes. It works every time. The hedgehog is supremely good at one thing, and it survives by sticking to its winning strategy. Identifying your own enterprise's Hedgehog Strategy flows from a thorough and objective understanding of what you can (and cannot) be world-class at.

The 95:5 Rule

When searching for opportunities and threats, the knack is to pick out the important few from the trivial many, because here, as elsewhere, the Pareto Principle applies. Based on economist Wilfredo Pareto's observation that 80% of the wealth was owned by 20% of the population in Italy at the time, the Pareto Principle is also known as the '80:20 Rule'. I find it's usually more of a **95:5 Rule**.

95:5 Rule

The 95:5 Rule describes the way that an important few things are responsible for most of the impact on events. For example 95% of sales can come from 5% of products. 95% of profits can come from 5% of customers. Or 95% of your competitive advantage could be derived from just 5% of your strengths. (Also, 95% of headaches are caused by 5% of colleagues!) Etcetera...

recognise your strengths and weaknesses in relation to your competitors

Continuing Professional Development

Ideas in Action — see page 86

Weaknesses may be plentiful and can be found in any area of the PRIMEFACT checklist. The good news is that they don't all need to be fixed. Playing to your strengths also includes playing away from your weaknesses. Your business formula includes deciding what *not* to do. Only weaknesses which could jeopardise your business strategy need to be rectified. *See Chapter 11: Your Route to Success.*

Skills: Training or Learning ?

There are many more ways of learning than attending training courses. As well as recognising your enterprise's key skills (core competencies), there will be areas where skills need to be improved, and given the changing external environment and changing needs of customers, constant learning is inevitably an ingredient of success. A training needs analysis can be undertaken to assess the gaps in skills and knowledge essential to the business strategy, though personally I prefer to focus on 'learning needs' rather than 'training needs'. Learning is much wider than training. A culture of encouraging learning is much more important than a budget for training.

Lifelong learning is not just a buzzword but a fact of life and a programme of **Continuing Professional Development** (CPD) is essential for all individuals playing a part in the enterprise to ensure that their skills and knowledge are kept up to date for the benefit of the business and its customers. Each person could have a Personal Development Portfolio or plan (PDP), as do staff members at The Team.

The Learning Organisation

Learning Organisation

Ideas in Action — see page 86

At a corporate level there needs to be a philosophy of building a **Learning Organisation**, which I describe as a company or other institution within which everybody continuously learns: from customers, from the competition and from colleagues. See The Team. Just as important is a culture where this learning is shared with colleagues and through systems this knowledge is embedded within the organisation as 'structural intellectual capital'. This is the know-how in the firm which is more than the sum total of individuals' expertise and belongs to the organisation rather than (or as well as) the people working within it.

Business Dashboard
see page 99

In a creative enterprise, constant learning and the build-up of knowledge should be part of a **Business Dashboard** and monitored as closely as financial measures of success. Crucially, the priorities for learning must be aligned to the overall business strategy, rather than individuals' personal preferences.

‘
learning
is
much
wider
than
training
’

Key Points

1   Assess the strengths and weaknesses of yourself and your business, including all stakeholders.

2   Use the PRIMEFACT checklist.

3   Ask outsiders to help – they may see weaknesses and strengths you don't.

4   Remember that not all weaknesses need to be fixed.

5   Identify the core competencies at the root of your success.

6   Think of the hedgehog's strategy to find out what you can be world-class at.

7   Use the 95:5 Rule to identify the most important 5% of your strengths and weaknesses.

8   Identify the additional learning and skills needs required to support the business strategy.

9   A culture of encouraging learning is much more important than a budget for training.

10 There are many more ways of learning than attending training courses. Think 'learning' rather than 'training' so as to open new possibilities for increasing knowledge and skills.

Ideas in Action

Peppered Sprout / Plastic Rhino
Advertising

"We liked the product so much, we shredded it." This was (almost) what Chris Morris said when he was telling me about how they set out to win new business from Puma UK for his company Peppered Sprout. Chris and business partner Peter Kellett decided that Puma was one of their target clients and decided to impress them with their outrageous creativity, publishing photos of Puma shoes shredded into hairpieces in their magazine *Plastic Rhino*. They won the account.

Deliberately following in the footsteps of David Ogilvy, founder of world-famous advertising agency Ogilvy and Mather, Chris doesn't fit the stereotype of the striped shirt and braces Manhattan executive. His casual clothes and easy manner disguise a shrewd business brain. Like David Ogilvy, Chris and Peter have a target list of clients they intend to work with and they actively pursue them. They don't advertise. They don't do tendering. They go for the jugular.

Plastic Rhino, their magazine, was originally "a folly", confesses this advertising man, but in practice it has turned out to be the most effective way of promoting themselves – a showcase for the ideas generated by their 8 staff and international database of freelance artists. With distribution in 15 countries, *Plastic Rhino* is a success in its own right.

"The best thing we did was to set out our stall," says Chris as he told me how he and Peter worked out clear aims for the business in the early days. They had been publishers and could have focused on publishing *Plastic Rhino*, defining their business as publishing. Instead they recognised that their core competencies are in delivering ideas to clients and the magazine is just one manifestation of that capability. And so it sits under the umbrella of Peppered Sprout which provides advertising for clients through in-store installations, photography and illustration, packaging and bespoke publishing.

The team at Peppered Sprout know where they're going, play to their strengths, are clear about what business they are in, and which clients they intend to win to develop their creative enterprise in the chosen direction.

www.pepperedsprout.com

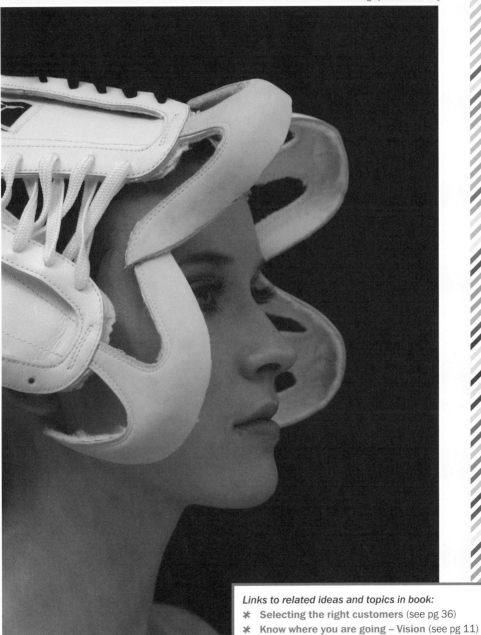

Photograph: Mark McNulty

Links to related ideas and topics in book:
* **Selecting the right customers** (see pg 36)
* **Know where you are going – Vision** (see pg 11)
* **Recognise Core Competencies** (see pg 19)
* **Mix of employees and freelancers** (see pg 84)

3

Keeping a Lookout

— This chapter outlines the benefits of using a business 'radar' to monitor the changing world for opportunities and threats which could affect your enterprise for better or worse.

Watch out! There's stuff going on out there that can make or break your business. It's a rapidly changing world and the changes taking place are outside our direct control – changes in technology, economics and regulations for example. Such changes in the external environment can have dramatic effects on businesses and organisations, indeed on whole industries.

Mobile phones have altered the way we communicate in the last few years, the Internet has opened up global markets. European Union regulations affect a growing number of national governments and every citizen living inside its expanding borders. Change is constant.

Using 'Radar'

To stay ahead of the game we need to anticipate changes, not just react to them. This requires constant 'scanning' of the external environment and I liken this to a ship's radar, constantly looking out for both hazards and help, picking up on its radar screens approaching ships and impending storms in good time. Naturally, we are in touch with the world we live in and we constantly learn about new developments from TV, friends, publications and a host of other sources. But to have an effective 360° **Business Radar**, it pays to be more systematic in scanning for opportunities – and threats. This scanning can be called an **External Audit** (or Environmental Analysis). A **PEST Analysis** simply invites us to look in four directions: political, economic, social and technological for threats and opportunities. A more thorough approach is to look in eight directions using the **ICEDRIPS checklist** overleaf, an acronym I invented which I have used with many organisations to help them identify opportunities and threats to their businesses or social enterprises. See The Windows Project.

‘
*stay
ahead
of
the
game*
’

Business Radar

ICEDRIPS checklist

Ideas in Action — see page 102

The ICEDRIPS checklist

Ideas in Action — see page 32

Innovations
include computer technology and the Internet (of course) but other developments in the biosciences and transportation.

Forces of Competition
see page 47

Competition
not only from rivals but threats from other **Forces of Competition** such as new entrants and substitute products.

Economics
includes factors such as inflation, exchange rates, downturns in the industry, public spending etc.

Demographics
include the ageing of the population, migration, trends in employment, social class etc.

Ideas in Action — see pages 78, 102

Regulations
such as new laws, protocols, agreements, conventions and industry regulations eg Ofcom regulations and school inspections via Ofsted.

Infrastructure
such as telecommunications networks, transport, public services and utilities.

Partners
Strategic alliances with other companies or organisations (see also Co-opetition).

Co-opetition
see page 48

Social trends
including acceptance of technology, use of leisure time, fashions and changing beliefs.

The factors above are not in order of importance, the checklist merely provides an easy to remember acronym.

The best way to use the checklist is to produce a long list of 100 or so things going on in the world – and things likely to happen. (Imagine all the things you would have to tell a colleague who'd been in outer space for ten years!)

This will produce a generic list, useful for all organisations. The Competition and Partners elements will apply more specifically to the business or organisation in question.

Then add any special external factors relevant to your sector. This might include technical developments, government initiatives or industry matters for example.

Write all of them down and then sift carefully through them for the factors that could represent opportunities and threats for your business.

For example, low-cost international flights (infrastructure) and downloadable music files (innovation) provide opportunities for some enterprises, whilst on the other hand the increasing possibility of litigation (regulations) and new entrants to the market from new European states (competition) represent threats for other businesses.

Depending on your position, changes can produce progress or disaster; changes can be forces for good or bad depending on how they affect you; changes can present either opportunities or threats, depending on how you deal with them. For example, the Disability Discrimination Act in the UK affects architects, web designers, advertisers and other creative businesses. Whilst some will see it as a problem for their businesses, those who are 'ahead of the game' will adapt to new requirements quickly and gain competitive advantage.

Remember that there are other **Forces of Competition** as well as your immediate rivals, including the relative power of buyers and suppliers as well as new entrants and substitute products, that can present either opportunities or threats, depending on how you manoeuvre in the changing competitive environment.

‘ *changes can present either opportunities or threats* ’

Forces of Competition
see page 47

On the other hand, apparent competitors can become co-operators in certain circumstances, transforming rivals into partners and threats into opportunities, using the idea of **Co-opetition**.

Co-opetition
see page 48

Timothy Chan, Chairman of Shanghai-based computer games manufacturer Shanda Entertainment, operates in a culture where pirating software is rife. Software pirating was a threat but he turned it into an opportunity when Shanda changed their business model so that clients have to pay to play games online. So the distribution of pirate copies of the software actually encourages more people to log on and become paying customers.[12]

Ideas in Action — see page 32

Online Originals took advantage of changes in the external environment (especially Innovation) to launch the very first Internet-only e-book publishing venture.

Having used the checklist to identify as many positive and negative factors, the next step is to identify the important few of each, using the **95:5 Rule**. It may be just 5% of external opportunities that lead to 95% of your future success. Just one major threat could be twenty times more significant than several other threats identified.

95:5 Rule
see page 20

As for threats, anticipate the worst possibilities – then decide how to deal with them or avoid them. See also **Risk Analysis**.

Risk Analysis
see page 100

The counterpart of Risk Analysis is **Opportunity Analysis**. Using similar principles as Risk Analysis, Opportunity Analysis is the technique of assessing which opportunities are most likely to present business benefits, and the possible positive impact of each of them, in order to prioritise the most significant opportunities.

In conclusion, the ICEDRIPS checklist enables you to devise your **Business Radar** as an early warning system to avoid or defend against threats whilst identifying emerging opportunities before your competitors do.

Business Radar
see page 27

Key Points

1 External forces beyond our control can affect our businesses positively or negatively.

2 We need to anticipate changes, not just react to them.

3 Use the ICEDRIPS checklist as a 'business radar' to scan the external environment for forces that could affect your enterprise.

4 Sift the external environment for the one or two special opportunities – and for potential threats.

5 Threats can be turned into opportunities.

6 Remember the 95:5 Rule and separate the important few from the trivial many.

7 Anticipate the worst possibilities – then decide how to deal with them or avoid them.

8 Constantly keep a lookout.

Ideas in Action

Online Originals
Internet Publisher of Electronic Books

Online Originals, the world's first Internet-only e-book publisher, took advantage of several changes in the technological environment to become the pioneer of Internet e-book publishing. They were responsible for many 'firsts' in the sector: the use of PDF files as the standard format for e-books; the issuing of ISBN numbers for e-books; and reviews of e-books in the mainstream press. They also published the first e-book to be nominated for the Booker Prize. Their list includes original works of book-length fiction, non-fiction and drama.

In 1995, David Gettman and co-founder Christopher Macann saw an opportunity for a new kind of publishing venture, taking advantage of the Internet as an ecommerce distribution channel to readers using PCs, Apple Macs and Palm personal digital assistants to read digital files of their authors' works.

At a time when most published authors were locked into contracts with traditional publishers which excluded electronic publishing rights, Online Originals were quick-witted and agile enough to negotiate 'electronic rights only' deals with authors, including best-selling writer Frederick Forsyth. This arrangement leaves authors free to negotiate other contracts with conventional book publishers.

Online Originals redefined publishing and created a new business model which cuts out most of the costs associated with traditional publishing including printing, warehousing, physical distribution and the remaindering of unsold stock, based instead almost entirely on intangible assets. This new 'business formula' makes it economically feasible to publish short print run titles that would not be commercially attractive to the publishing conglomerates. What's more, their new economic formula pays a full 50% of net sales income as royalties to authors, who retain copyright in their works.

Whilst traditional publishers are wary of the potential of e-books to undermine sales of paper copies, as an electronic-only publisher Online Originals takes a different view. Encryption technology is rejected for both philosophical and business reasons, encouraging the sharing of digital books between friends, which acts as a form of viral marketing spreading the word about Online Originals itself as the e-book is passed from one reader to another.

With the help of venture capital investment, Online Originals now use the latest technology to automate many of the business processes of publishing – even the handling of manuscript submissions and their reviews. This automates their unique peer-review system for submissions, whereby the community of current authors serves as the 'gateway' for admitting new titles. It's also a virtual organisation (there's no mention here about where it's located because it doesn't matter) which does its business mainly in cyberspace, without the need for corporate headquarters, storage facilities or retail outlets.

www.onlineoriginals.com

Being and Becoming, Volume 1   Christopher Macann

being for others falls apart into a dichotomy. However, this divergence of being *for itself* and being *for others* does not mean that the self recovers a sense of itself, and so comes to know itself as it is for itself. Rather, the rejection of the point of view of the other takes the form, initially, of an objectification of the self, that is, a positing of the self as it is not for this that or the other Other but for all others in general, that is, for all those selves which are capable of taking up with regard to themselves the point of view of an other. In positing its self as an object of knowledge, the self becomes oblivious of the fact that it is itself the very subject who objectifies, or rather, who has already objectified itself. This objectification of the self by itself takes the form of an objectification of the psyche, on the one hand, and of behaviour, on the other.

The *psyche* is that which any self is for itself in so far as it is a mind. *Behaviour* is that which any self is for others in so far as it is a body. Thus, in coming to understand what it is 'in itself', the self actually only objectifies the dual mode of being for itself and being for others, that dual mode which was initially united by the identification of the self with what it is for others.

The objectification of the self by itself is however a contradictory project. For, in the course of objectifying itself, the subject makes itself be what it is not, namely an object, and this in the dual mode of a psyche and a behavioural complex. Actually, neither the objectification of the psyche nor that of behaviour is possible without the surreptitious introduction of both a subjective and an objective component. The psyche is the internality of the self, the manifestation of the self to itself. In consequence, the objectification of the psyche involves an objectification of the subject by itself. Behaviour, on the other hand, is the

318

Being and Becoming, Volume 1   Christopher Macann

externality of the self, the manifestation of the self to others. But the investigation of behaviour could not take the form of an investigation of the self if this behaviour was not taken to be something more than, or other than, a physical event. Just as the analysis of the psyche assumes the form of a tacit objectification of mental events, so the analysis of behaviour assumes the form of a tacit 'subjectification' of the physical movements of the body. Through just such a surreptitious exchange, as between the two modalities of subjectification and objectification, the contradiction involved in the project of cognitive self-knowledge gets covered over, with the result that both the psyche and behaviour get set up as legitimate and self-contained domains of objective enquiry. We shall consider each of these two domains in turn with a view to determining the kind of self-knowledge which follows therefrom.

Before we enter into an examination of the psyche, we should first take note of an equivocation which lies at the root of the very conception of a psyche. The psyche is an 'internal' object, consisting essentially of mental states and their contents. So far from being called in question, the internality of the mind is simply taken for granted as an intrinsic characteristic of the subject, that very subject which undertakes the project of objectification. And yet, as we have seen, the objectivity of the empirical object manifests itself in the three characteristics of identity, publicity and normality, of which the latter two at least run counter to the postulate of internality. The empirical object must be so constituted as to be experientially accessible to any subject under all normal circumstances. As an empirical object, albeit an object of a distinctive kind, the psyche must also conform to the norms of empirical objectivity. How then is the internality of the psychic object to be rendered

319

Links to related ideas and topics in book:

* **External Environment** (see pg 27)
* **Virtual Organisation** (see pg 75)
* **Copyright** (see pg 54)
* **Intangible Assets** (see pg 53)
* **Viral Marketing** (see pg 40)

The Magic of Marketing

— This chapter explains that the real meaning of marketing is not about advertising and selling but choosing the right customers in the first place, then being prepared to put them at the centre and build your business around their requirements, listen to them and respond to their changing needs.

'Marketing' isn't just a posh word for 'selling'. It's much more radical than that. Marketing in its widest and best sense is about aligning your whole business to the changing needs of your customers.

The Marketing Problem

Oscar Wilde wrote: "The play was a great success but the audience was a total failure." Some people tell me their business is fine – the problem is the customers! Usually a lack of them. The 'marketing problem' they claim to have is that they cannot convince people to buy their things. Their real problem is that their business is built around themselves and their products or services, not around customers' needs. They do their thing in a customer-free zone, a kind of creative vacuum. They are product-focused, not customer-focused. Then they hope that some marketing magic will sell it. It's as if they believe marketing is a kind of magic dust that clever marketers can sprinkle onto any old product or service to make it sell like hot cakes to anyone.

Successful creative enterprises are truly customer-focused, not in the sense of putting customers in their sights (as if firing products at them), but putting the customer at the centre of their universe so that their entire business revolves around them. It's a fundamentally different philosophy.

It's a shift of thinking, from **How can we sell what we want to create?** to **How can we use our creativity to provide what customers want to buy?**

The word 'marketing' encompasses both science and art as well as a wide range of skills, but essentially it can be separated into strategic marketing and operational marketing.

successful creative enterprises are truly customer focused

35

Selecting the right customers

Strategic and Operational Marketing

Operational marketing is the more visible side: advertising, PR and selling that is about communicating towards customers, telling them about products and services. Strategic marketing concerns itself with deciding what products and services to produce in the first place, based on customers' changing needs. It is responsible for aligning the whole organisation around the needs of particular customers. It's crucial that strategic marketing comes first because unless your initial business formula is right – matching particular products and services with selected customers profitably – then operational marketing will fail, no matter how clever (or creative) the advertising.

The strategic marketing formula includes decisions about which customers to serve. This is not a matter of opportunism but at the heart of your business formula and route to success.

Customer Focus

Selecting the right customers in the first place is an essential element of any successful business formula. Then organising your enterprise around the changing needs of these selected clients or market segments is what marketing really means. In other words, putting customers first – at the beginning of the business process, not at the end. **Customers' needs have to be the whole point of the business from beginning to end.** That's why David Packard co-founder of Hewlett Packard famously said: "Marketing is too important to be left just to the marketing department." Marketing is the responsibility of the whole business, not just the sales people at the end of the line.

The most strategically focused businesses have a list of target clients that they have identified as fitting in with their business strategy. David Ogilvy, founder of advertising agency Ogilvy and Mather wrote in his book *Confessions of an Advertising Man* how he built up his business by targeting clients and focused on getting their accounts at all costs. Ogilvy and Mather's client list over 50 years includes names such as American Express, Ford, Shell, Barbie, Kodak, IBM, Dove and Maxwell

Ideas in Action
— see pages 14, 24 & 94

House. For examples of other creative businesses that have targeted specific customers see Sharon Mutch, Peppered Sprout and the Mando Group.

Marketing is definitely not a matter of trying to 'please all the customers all the time', but selecting the customers you can partner with most effectively and profitably, matching their needs with your creative skills. Just as business strategy includes deciding what not to do, strategic marketing includes deciding which customers not to deal with. Not all customers are good customers. Trying to focus on every possible customer is not being focused at all!

Segmenting the Market

Market Segmentation

Market Segmentation is the process of dividing potential customers into groups with similar characteristics – perhaps geography, gender, age, needs, industry, or whatever is most useful or relevant. Analysing customer segments allows clear decisions to be made about prioritising target segments and deciding which types of customers to avoid because they do not fit the specification of your business formula. It can also help with operational marketing as each segment's similar characteristics can help to identify the most effective media channels to use to approach each group. One particularly useful way of segmenting customers is based on the media they read and watch, since this also automatically indicates which advertising media to use.

Existing customers are a useful resource, because analysing their characteristics can help you understand which market segments you can work with best. Despite the strategic approach advocated here, your customer base may have developed more by accident than by design. And your current customers may help you to understand your business strengths and weaknesses – if you ask them. *See Chapter 2: Know Yourself.*

Furthermore, it's easier and cheaper (up to five times as much, it is said) to win more business from existing clients compared to winning new customers. Take care of them!

Focusing on old customer

In addition, existing customers can be the route to new clients. Word of mouth is the best advertising (and the cheapest) so encourage it to happen if it leads to the right kind of customer.

Listening to Customers

Listening to customers

So if customers are the whole point of the business, from beginning to end, it's clearly not enough simply to talk at them at the end, but to listen to them from the beginning. Marketing is a dialogue, not a monologue. **Listening to customers** has many dimensions but it is primarily an attitude towards customers as active partners, not passive targets. This involves looking at things from the customers' point of view.

Marketing can be described as 'being close to the customer' and it includes **market research** but not only the stereotypical market research (which makes me think of avoiding eye contact with people carrying clipboards in the high street and those annoying unwanted phone calls when I'm watching TV). There are many ways of listening to customers and looking at things from the customers' point of view if you want to. If you really want to know about markets and customers, you can find out through various means, indirect and direct. As well as direct (primary) research, market research also includes secondary (desk) research using published data from industry analyses, government statistics and trade journals, much of which is available in libraries or on the Internet. See Sharon Mutch.

Ideas in Action — see page 14

More directly you can visit customers, invite them to focus groups, and watch them use your product (or a competitor's). Visit them to see how they work. Get customers involved in new product development as New Mind do. Explore how you can help their businesses develop. Last but not least, listen to them and establish a dialogue through feedback mechanisms, focus groups, suggestions boxes, or over a lunch. Buy them a drink and get to know them. In return you'll get their good ideas and loyalty.

Ideas in Action — see page 42

> look at things from the customers' point of view

Sometimes insights emerge about what customers are really buying, which may not be what you think you are selling them. For example the apocryphal tales of the beer that was bought only because the empty can made an excellent oil lamp in Africa; the bookstore that found nobody returned the voucher placed deep inside the Booker Prize-winning novel because in reality people bought it to leave on their coffee table to impress their friends. Such unsettling observations help you to see things from the customer's point of view.

Ask yourself: What do you know about your current customers, lost customers and target customers? **What would you ideally like to know?** Devise a way of finding out.

Operational Marketing

If you get your strategic marketing right, then operational marketing becomes much easier. In other words, if you have devised a business formula around a natural fit between selected customers and the products they want, at the right price, then advertising and promotion becomes more a matter of informing them rather than coercing them. There's no need for cold calling or hard selling if you've listened to customers all along and they've been included in the project from the start. On the other hand, even the most persuasive (or 'creative') advertising will not sell a product if it's not what the customers want and at the right price.

Four Ps of Marketing

Product

Price

Promotion

Place

The Marketing Mix is a blend of the **Four Ps of Marketing**: Product, Price, Promotion and Place. (Place really means Distribution but '3 Ps and a D' doesn't have the same ring to it.) These four controllable elements can be blended in different ways to maximise sales – so long as the product is right for the carefully selected target market.

Promotion is actually just one aspect of the marketing mix but it's what people often mean when they use the term 'marketing' as shorthand for advertising, public relations (PR) or other channels of marketing communications including direct mail and attending trade shows. All of these are essentially about getting the right message to the right people in the most effective way, emphasising **benefits not features.**

Benefits not features
see page 47

Ideas in Action — see page 94

Viral Marketing

Ideas in Action — see page 32

Operational marketing is always limited by budgets and that budget can be very small indeed, especially for new creative businesses. Sometimes, however, the cheapest is the best – word of mouth recommendations for example – so encourage this to happen and reward it when it does. Mando Group gives a percentage commission for recommendations that lead to new work. **Viral Marketing**, used extremely effectively by Hotmail to advertise itself at the bottom of messages as emails zoom around the Internet is also used by Online Originals as their e-books are sent between friends sharing works of literature.

By adopting an attitude to customers as partners rather than passive targets, interactive forms of marketing come to mind. For example websites that people can engage with (not just read) and printed materials that invite a response all treat customers as active participants.

Rather than thinking of expensive and relatively untargeted mass marketing (which in any case would be inappropriate for most creative businesses) turn this approach on its head and decide which single customer would be perfect if you could only have one. Then track down this ideal customer, then find one more, then another and so on.

In conclusion, marketing is not a magic dust that can make anything sell. The magic of marketing works when you put customers at the centre and build your enterprise around their needs.

Key Points

1   Marketing is not just a posh word for selling.
   It's much more radical than that.

2   Sort out your strategic marketing (part of your business
   formula) before planning your operational marketing.

3   Target specific market segments or specific customers.
   Draw up a target list of clients to win.

4   Marketing is a dialogue, not a monologue. It includes
   listening to customers as well as talking to them.

5   Not all customers are good customers.
   Decide which are good and bad for your enterprise.

6   Are you truly customer-focused or still product-focused?

7   Build your business around customers' changing needs.
   Be prepared to change as customers' needs do.

8   How much do you know about your current customers,
   lost customers and target customers? What would you
   like to know? Devise a way of finding out what you need
   to know, through various means including direct and
   indirect market research.

9   Help and encourage existing customers to recommend
   you to new customers – so long as they are the right kind.

10 Define the ideal customer then find one.
   Then another one, and so on.

Ideas in Action

New Mind Internet
Internet, Marketing and Technology

"Identify a market segment and make it your own" is Richard Veal's advice to other creative entrepreneurs and that's what New Mind has done with its specialist software for the tourism sector. "A world class product in a niche market", Richard also describes it as "a piece of software that works for clients". One of the reasons it works so well is that customers are involved in its development and new versions of the software are released every three months to keep pace with clients' evolving needs. New Mind listens to its customers and concentrates its creativity and skills on delivering solutions that deliver results.

In contrast to the company's Iomis® product, which is aimed at a more general market, its tourism software has no generic brand but is a 'white label' product, enabling clients to badge it with their own brand. So for example it is known by the Lancashire Tourist Authority as 'LOIS', the Lancashire Online Information System and by The Mersey Partnership as 'MERVIN' the Merseyside Visitor Information Network.

Founded in 1999 by Richard and business partner Andy Abram, the New Mind Group has 30 employees and a turnover in excess of £2m. Its rapid growth of 1000% in 5 years earned the business the prestigious 'Inner City 100' award for fastest growing business in the North West. New Mind's technology and websites have also won awards for several of its clients, the portfolio of which includes Bath Tourism and The Beatles Story, plus many others.

The New Mind Group is incorporated as three separate companies: New Mind Technology Ltd, New Mind Internet Consultancy Ltd and New Mind Marketing Ltd. This is partly to provide separate branding for their range of work and also to distribute business risk. New Mind Internet Consultancy employs the Group's 30 members of staff and most of the Group's business is conducted through this company. Quite deliberately, the Group's intellectual property belongs to New Mind Technology Ltd, which would allow the Group to sell its intellectual property at a later date through the sale of this company, with the benefits of it having no employees and providing a tax-efficient means of selling its valuable intangible assets.

www.newmind.co.uk

Richard (left) and Andy, New Mind Internet

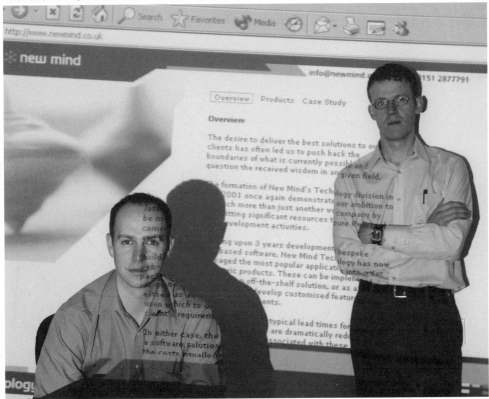

Links to related ideas and topics in book:
* **Exploitation of Intellectual Property** (see pg 58)
* **Company Structures** (see pg 75)
* **Customer involvement in the development of products** (see pg 38)
* **Customers' changing needs** (see pg 36)

5

Dealing with Competition

— In this chapter we look at Ideas about how to deal with competitors and position yourself amongst them to create a competitive advantage.

— We also look at the larger forces of competition, including new entrants and substitute products as well as your immediate rivals.

— Finally the idea of co-operating with the competition – 'co-opetition'.

As well as focusing on customers' changing needs, the most successful creative businesses recognise they are working in a competitive environment and devise a competitive strategy. Other businesses are in the market for the same customers too! Some enterprises will compete on price whilst others specialise to serve a niche market, becoming the best in that niche and charging premium prices to match.

Competitive Advantage

One of the questions to answer is: What can we do better than our competitors? Ironically this might not be what you are best at! **Competitive Advantage** is found in that area where you beat your competitors hands-down – even if it's not your best skill, or the thing you enjoy the most. *handmade*

The analogy I use here is about my fell running. I run faster downhill than uphill (obviously) but so does everyone else! Running uphill is slower and more painful – but it is for my competitors too. In the uphill stage I finish nearer the front of the pack but I'm slower than average running down. So maybe I should compete in Italy where fell races finish at the top, because there my combination of strengths and weaknesses would give me a competitive advantage.

Thinking about competitive advantage in this way and focusing on customers' needs at the same time, the question becomes: **Which customers' problems can we solve better than anyone else?**

Business strategy – your route to success – involves deciding what specifically to do, and with which customers. It also involves deciding what **not** to do, including deciding which market segments not to compete in because the competition is too strong, concentrating instead on areas where you have competitive advantage. **Selecting the right customers** needs to be done in the context of competitors.

Competitive Advantage

which customers' problems can we solve better than anyone else?

Selecting the right customers
see page 36

You and Your Rivals

Competitive Positioning

Competitive Positioning is the technique of analysing where you currently fit in amongst competing businesses, deciding where you should be and identifying your own 'high ground' on the competitive battlefield.

What is your customers' perception of your business in relation to your rivals?

You and your competitors can be plotted on graphs with various axes, such as price, service level, speed etc. A technique known as **charting the competition**[13] allocates scores against, say, ten key criteria for each of your competitors as well as yourself. This helps to establish where you can position yourself and where you need to improve.

Charting the competition

Customers' perspectives are paramount here and it's vital to look at your business – and the others – from the customers' point of view. Customers will label you or your rivals as 'cheap and cheerful', 'most expensive but worth the money', being 'easy to deal with', having the 'fastest turnaround' or whatever they define as 'quality'.

Quality

Everyone is in favour of quality – but what exactly does it mean? More to the point, whose definition of quality is more important – yours or the customer's? The National Library for the Blind (NLB), publisher of books in Braille format, prides itself on the high quality of its flawless Braille. It's a skilled process that can take months. By listening to its readers, NLB found that some customers preferred to read unchecked Braille proofs, available just days after the publication of the printed original, rather than wait several weeks for the perfect item. For them, speed was a quality issue. Now the NLB lets its readers choose which type of quality they want.

Quality is not a fixed thing. In business terms quality is a harmony between customers' needs and what's provided.

Forces of Competition

💡 **Forces of Competition**

The most obvious competition comes from the other guys who do the same thing as you, but these are merely your rivals, according to Professor Michael Porter[14] of Harvard Business School. There are four other **Forces of Competition** to take into account. These are New Entrants, Substitute Products and Services, the Bargaining Power of Suppliers and the Bargaining Power of Customers.

The question to ask in relation to new entrants is: What's to stop someone else setting up in business and competing directly with us? The 'barriers to entry' may be flimsy, unless your enterprise is founded on copyright-protected technology or designs, needs special licences or requires massive capital investment. How can you move into a position where others cannot easily follow?

entrepreneurs focus on customer benefits, not features

An even more potentially devastating competitive force is the substitute product. Remember what affordable word processors did to the typewriter industry! Who goes to New York by ocean liner in the age of the plane? Again, looking at it from the customer's point of view, what they want is not a typewriter or word processor but the ability to produce a professional document; not a berth in a ship or a seat on a plane, but to arrive safely and quickly in New York.

In terms of potential substitute products, the question here is: What is the benefit that the customer gets *from* existing products and services? A real understanding of customers' needs make you more likely to invent the substitute product or service yourself – rather than become the victim of it.

💡 **Benefits not features**

Entrepreneurs focus on customer **benefits not features** of the equipment or service that provides it. The customer wants to know "What's in it for me?". If the customer's response is "So what?", then you've been talking features, not benefits.

'
businesses
do
not
have
to
fail
for
others
to
succeed
'

Co-opetition

Sometimes competitors can also co-operate as partners in projects or joint ventures. **Co-opetition**[15] is the result of bringing together competition and co-operation to form not just a new word but also a new partnership.

A co-opetition partnership is more likely when your competitive positioning is different in some way, ie your specialities and strengths are not exactly the same.

Co-opetition is founded on the concept that businesses do not have to fail for others to succeed. They can co-operate to enlarge the pie then compete to carve it up, each getting more than they had before. Think of London's Charing Cross Road where booksellers compete alongside each other but at the same time combine to attract more customers to their world-class street of bookshops. Motor racing's Formula 1 industry is centred on a cluster of small specialist firms in the south of England. Similarly, 'creative clusters' in Liverpool, London, Helsinki, Huddersfield, Tokyo, Dublin, St Petersburg and Los Angeles attract customers by bringing together a concentration of related businesses which both compete and collaborate with each other.

In a nutshell, competitive advantage is the result of selecting the customers and markets where you will be a winner. Astute choices arise from understanding your strengths and weaknesses in relation to other enterprises so that you can choose wisely whether to avoid, compete (or co-operate) with them. The winners will be the businesses who provide the quality that profitable customers want, better than anyone else.

Key Points

1   Assess the strengths and weaknesses of your rivals in relation to target customers. Decide which competition you can beat – and which you cannot.

2   Anticipate competitive threats from substitute products – invent them before someone else does.

3   Understand the customers' needs that the current product or service satisfies.
Engage in a dialogue with customers.

4   What's to stop other people setting up in business in competition against you? How can you move to a place where they cannot follow?

5   Chart the competition. Where do you sit amongst your rivals? Where else could you position yourself?

6   Ask: Which customers' needs can we serve better than anyone else?

7   What are customers' perceptions of your business in relation to your rivals?

8   If the customers' response is "So what?" then you've been talking features not benefits.

9   Are there circumstances in which you could collaborate with competitors? Think about Co-opetition.

10 Are you part of a creative cluster? Could you be?

Ideas in Action

ESP Multimedia
CD/DVD Authoring and Video/Audio Post-Production

ESP Multimedia Ltd is a new media development company, specialising in CD ROM and DVD authoring, and video/audio post-production work, owned by David Hughes and David Harry. Its impressive client list includes Warner Bros, BBC, Sky, Toyota, Smirnoff and Film Four.

Before setting up ESP, Dave Hughes co-composed the soundtrack for the film *Lock, Stock and Two Smoking Barrels* and soon afterwards found himself in Los Angeles working on films such as *The Bachelor* starring Renée Zellweger. Such high-profile projects are not always the most lucrative, says Dave. More 'commercial' projects, such as building Sky TV's music library are more profitable long term – and they are not always less creative, insists Dave.

David Harry was a member of 90s' chart dance act 'Oceanic' before turning his talents to multimedia as a developer and consultant.

ESP's business formula combines the highly creative projects with what Dave calls the "bread and butter" activities, ie smaller jobs which keep the money coming in between the major projects, for example authoring and duplicating DVDs and CDs.

ESP's CD duplicating business, originally a partnership, has now been brought inside the limited company, in order to reduce business risks for the owners. 'CDDuplicator.co.uk' is still a separate brand and now acts as what Dave calls a "front door" for clients, to introduce them into ESP's sophisticated range of technical specialisms and professional media services.

Another income stream is derived from royalties on copyrights. For the BBC TV series *Funland*, Dave Hughes has negotiated retaining his publishing rights in some DVD releases and any other sales of the programme following the broadcast of the series in the UK.

Despite their high-profile projects and extensive client list, Dave maintains that their creative enterprise is ultimately about quality of life – in other words, a 'lifestyle business'.

www.espmultimedia.com
www.cdduplicator.co.uk

A DISGRACE TO CRIMINALS EVERYWHERE.

LOCK, STOCK AND TWO SMOKING BARRELS

David Hughes at work

Links to related ideas and topics in book:

* **Partnership and Company structures** (see pg 75)
* **'Commercial' and 'Creative' not necessarily a conflict** (see pg 8)
* **Retention of copyright to create income streams** (see pg 58)
* **Brands** (see pg 53)
* **Lifestyle Business** (see pg 9)

6

Protecting your Creativity

— This chapter comments on the growing importance of intangible assets in the Age of Information.
— It talks about the importance of Intellectual Property and how to protect your ideas through copyright, design rights, trademarks and patents.
— Crucially, it discusses how to use intellectual property rights to turn your bright ideas into income streams.

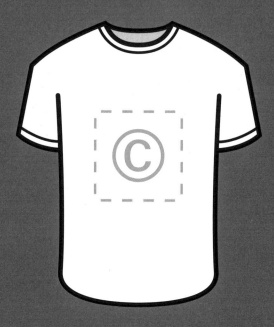

The new millennium heralded the 'Age of Information' and a transition from the industrial age as significant as the transformation to the industrial era from agricultural society a couple of centuries earlier. Correspondingly there was a shift in power and wealth from land to factories and from now on towards information and ideas.

The Age of Intangibles

This new era could be called the Age of Intangibles because so much power and wealth is becoming tied up in **intangible assets** such as brands, market information, know-how and ideas. Though we cannot touch them, intangibles can be bought and sold like land or machines and represent an increasing proportion of global wealth. If you buy a share in Microsoft, only a small fraction of what you are buying is in land, buildings and computer hardware; most of what you are buying into is a share of Microsoft's brands, licences, systems, expertise and morale of its employees – in other words the intangible stuff that will produce future profits. Conventional accountancy fails to find a good way of counting the value of intangibles, but the market takes it into account and is willing to pay far more than is represented on the balance sheet. It's a multi-billion dollar equivalent of paying extra for that invisible goodwill when buying a shop for more than the value of the premises plus its stock.

Intangible assets

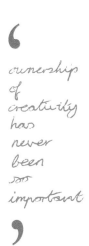

'ownership of creativity has never been so important'

Intellectual Property (IP)

Creative ideas have been around since well before someone designed and built the first wheel, but ownership of creativity has never been as clear-cut as ownership of natural resources or production facilities, and still isn't. For creative entrepreneurs living in the Age of Intangibles, ownership of creativity has never been so important. The ownership of creativity is complex, both philosophically and legally.

Intellectual Property (IP) is the product of creative ideas expressed in works and **Intellectual Property Rights (IPR)** are the legal powers associated with the ownership, protection and commercial exploitation of those creative works.

Intellectual Property is at the heart of the creative industries which have been defined as 'those activities which have their origin in individual creativity, skill and talent, and which have a potential for job and wealth creation through the generation and exploitation of intellectual property.'[16]

Copyright, Designs, Trademarks and Patents

This is a complex legal area but these main points should provide the basis for further research before seeking specialist advice.

In legal terms, ideas themselves cannot be owned, only their expression in a specific way. So the idea for a novel cannot be protected by copyright, only its written form. In UK law, copyright exists as soon as an idea is transformed into some permanent / tangible form. Registration is not necessary. Copyright automatically protects works including writing, music, film, artwork, broadcasts and computer programs. Generally copyright lasts for the lifetime of the author plus 70 years. The copyright symbol © is not essential, but indicates the copyright owner and that permission should be obtained to copy their work. Unregistered design right arises when a design is created, in a similar way to copyright. Designs can also be registered through the UK Patent Office so long as they have a unique 'individual character'.

Trademarks are used to distinguish the goods or services of one business from another. Trademarks are not only the logos that companies and organisations use as badges, but can also be words, shapes, pieces of music, smells or colours. (Cadbury's familiar purple colour is a registered trademark – nobody else can use the same colour for chocolate packaging.) Trademarks apply to different classes of goods and services which is why Penguin can be a trademark for both books and biscuits. Mimashima Records checked out

‘ ideas themselves cannot be owned ’

Ideas in Action — see page 60

trademarks globally before deciding their trading name. Though 'shima' was used by companies in Japan, none were record labels and so they were not infringing other companies' trademark rights. Medication is a registered trademark of a nightclub promoter, not a drug company.

Trademarks can be unregistered, or registered permanently through the UK Patent Office. Patents themselves are used to register and protect inventions and are mainly concerned with mechanisms, designs, processes etc.

The UK Patent Office website provides useful information and details of registering patents, designs and trademarks.

There is no obligation to register trademarks, designs or inventions – indeed the recipe for Coca Cola is protected by simple old-fashioned secrecy rather than a patent. Without registration, however, it will be more difficult to obtain legal protection if someone else uses your design, trademark or invention for their own purposes.

Intellectual Property Rights (IPR)

Intellectual Property Rights include moral rights, publishing rights and mechanical rights. Moral rights relate to the creator's rights to receive recognition as the creator of their work and to prevent others from falsely claiming credit for the creator's work. Copyright may remain with the creator of the work, or be transferred to another person or company. Publishing rights may be granted to a third party to publish a work in a particular way, for a limited duration, in specified markets, without transferring copyright to the publisher. The term 'mechanical rights' is used in the music industry and refers to a particular recording of a work. So the moral rights, copyright and mechanical rights in a piece of music may belong to three different people or companies. Copyrights, trademarks and other intellectual property can be bought and sold like other commodities. The rights and ownership of *Yesterday* and other Beatles songs is a story in itself.

'intellectual property can be bought and sold like other commodities'

In recent years the additional option of Internet downloads has created a new way to commercialise intellectual property. Rock legend Pete Wylie had the foresight to insist on keeping the download rights to his music when negotiating with his record company in 2000. His songs are now available for download from the iTunes Music Store and the resulting royalties are his.

David Bowie, both an artist and a businessman, put his creativity into commerce in 1997 and pioneered the sale of bonds to raise $55 million to buy back the copyrights in his music. He now controls the use of his works and repays bondholders a fixed rate of return on their investment from income generated by the exploitation of his intellectual property through numerous licensing deals.

Employees, Contractors and Clients

It's worth noting that an employee who creates something as part of their employment normally does so on behalf of their employer and so they do not own it themselves, the employer does. There should be a clear understanding between employer and employee about these issues, and this is normally set out in a contract of employment. New Mind's employees' contracts specify that the software they create belongs to the company. For freelance contractors and other situations the position is less clear cut and is negotiable. This is an important consideration in the business environment of the creative industries where there are so many freelance contractors and ad hoc partnerships as well as conventional employer-employee relationships. When engaged by a client to produce a creative product, ownership and future use of the fruits of creativity needs to be agreed in advance so the position is clear to all parties involved. The ownership and transfer of IP should be written into client contracts and terms of trade. See JAB Design.

Ideas in Action — see page 70

So intangibles can be protected to some extent, but ownership of their means of production is virtually impossible. Food is the product of land somebody owns and goods the product of a factory owned by a firm, but ideas are the product of a brain belonging to a person who cannot be owned and can walk

> *a creative enterprise's wealth is more likely to lie in its intangible assets*

Ideas in Action — see page 42

away from the business. If all your employees won the lottery jackpot in a syndicate and didn't return to work on Monday (it happened in Spain!) what value would be left in your creative enterprise? Land or factories cannot just walk away, but your human assets can.

What you have left in the business when all the employees have gone home is really all that you own. Only those things that are not dependent on individuals belong to the business itself. These tangible assets probably amount to not much more than office furniture, computers and some equipment. A creative enterprise's wealth is more likely to lie in its intangible assets, ie in its intellectual property such as copyrights, brands, trademarks and patents, appropriately registered and protected.

Generating ideas is the everyday work of creative and cultural enterprises and the expression of those ideas creates intellectual property. *Protecting* that intellectual property through the registration of trademarks, designs and patents prevents unfair exploitation of your creations so that you remain in business. Owning intellectual property that becomes an intangible asset underpins the value of your enterprise so that your business remains beyond you.

When you want to move on or retire, this is all you have to sell, because if the enterprise is entirely based on your skills and what's in your head, your business cannot be sold to someone else. New Mind put all their intellectual property into one of their companies so that it could be sold separately in the future.

Turning Creativity into Cashflow

Whilst moral rights give recognition to the artist or creator, in business terms the point of intellectual property rights is to utilise (exploit) them to create revenue streams for their owner through direct sales and licensing agreements.

Many creative businesses view the whole area of intellectual property purely defensively, simply to protect their rights. Successful creative entrepreneurs also have an assertive approach. I will use a metaphor from the world of tangible products, for example goods stacked in a warehouse. Yes, we need to lock them securely away at night to protect them from thieves. But during the day we need to open our doors widely and confidently to sell our wares. That's when we make our money. Whilst we need to protect our intellectual property from theft, we must also look for opportunities to sell it, which cannot be done if the focus is so much on protection that the doors are permanently locked.

Creative work can be repurposed, ie expressed in different ways through a range of saleable items. So for example an artist can sell not only the original work but also prints, postcards or even mugs and mouse mats.

Ideas in Action — see page 78

The Red Production Company licenses format rights and sells DVDs of its TV productions.

Licence agreements allow third parties to use intellectual property, for specific purposes and periods of time, in exchange for fees, without selling the intellectual property rights. For example David Hughes has licence agreements with the BBC. See ESP Multimedia.

Ideas in Action — see page 50

In conclusion...
the business of creativity is the art of turning recognition into reward,
and the science of turning intellectual property into income streams.

Key Points

1   Count your intangible assets as well as the tangible ones.

2   Assess your current intellectual assets as part of the PRIMEFACT analysis of your strengths and weaknesses.

3   Include your intellectual property – and its protection – in your business strategy.

4   Intellectual property should not only be protected but also exploited. How can you turn it into income directly or indirectly?

5   Are you sure you are not infringing on other people's intellectual property rights?

6   Are your contracts with employees, clients and contractors clear about the ownership and transfer of intellectual property rights?

7   A creative enterprise's wealth is more likely to lie in intangible assets than tangible ones.

8   What value do you have left in the business when all the employees have gone home?

9   Get expert advice on registering designs, trademarks and patents. How much value lies in the parts of your business that cannot just walk away?

10 Remember: the business of creativity is the art of turning recognition into reward and the science of turning intellectual property into income streams.

Ideas in Action

Medication
Student Club Night and Promotions Company

Medication® is the registered trademark of Medication Ltd – **not** a pharmaceuticals company but the promoters of Liverpool's most successful student night out.

Founder Marc Jones registered his brand as a trademark with the UK Patent Office under Class 41, which includes 'entertainment services; nightclub and discotheque services'.

Marc explained: "It would be impossible to register 'Medication' as a trademark for any kind of medical product, but that's not the business we are in, and there was no problem registering it for exclusive use as an entertainment brand."

Marc and brother Jason Jones plan to build the brand and diversity into merchandise including music publishing and clothing. By thinking ahead, they also registered Medication as a trademark in Class 09 (sound and video recordings in the form of discs or tapes) and Class 25 (clothing, footwear and headgear).

Medication is a business with no significant fixed assets and Marc and Jason recognise that their enterprise is based on their know-how and another intangible asset – their brand and registered trademark.

The protection of the enterprise's Intellectual Property through the registration of their brand as a trademark puts them in a position to expand their 'student night' business to other cities. The trademark registration in additional classes enables them to diversify the brand into other activities such as merchandising.

Furthermore, they are now in a strong position to negotiate joint ventures with other businesses hoping to capitalise on the 'Medication' brand. At the time of writing, Medication have just started a joint venture with Liquidation, one of Liverpool's leading alternative nights, called 'Indiecation' – a new Friday night that is looking to capture the nation's reawakened interest in big guitars, fuzzy amps and skinny boy and girl bands.

www.medication.co.uk

Links to related ideas and topics in book:

* **Intellectual Property** (see pg 54)
* **Trademarks** (see pg 54)
* **Intangible Assets** (see pg 53)
* **Brands** (see pg 53)

7
Counting Your Money

— This chapter emphasises the importance of understanding and monitoring your enterprise's financial health by looking at financial measures from three different perspectives.
— It also covers raising funds and the importance of generating future income streams both for investors and your own long-term financial security.

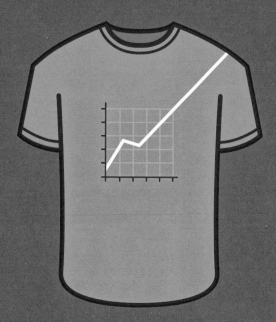

This financial section applies to not-for-profit organisations as well as commercial businesses. In fact in my own experience it sometimes requires more financial acumen to run a social enterprise, balancing creative or social ideals with economic pressures to achieve the required financial outcome.

When I ask businesses about their weaknesses, usually one of the first answers I receive is "we don't have enough money!" Clearly, a critical lack of cash is a problem for any business or social enterprise – new or established – and it can present barriers to thriving or even surviving.

The financial barriers are real – or sometimes imaginary. 'Imaginary' in the sense that people often *imagine* that to start a new business requires immediately having all the assets and trappings of a well-established enterprise: equipment, offices, vehicles etc, when very often it needs less than they think. The question is not so much: How much money would we like ideally? A better question is: How little do we need to make the enterprise feasible? (either a new business or an additional venture). Waiting for the day all the money arrives, from the bank, a funder, or the Lottery could mean it never happens. Success stories often start from meagre beginnings. Equipment can be hired or borrowed rather than bought new, vehicles rented, offices can be shared (or virtual) and professional services can be traded. Growth can be organic rather than a sudden step-change and managing on low overheads can be not only a useful discipline in the early days but also the basis of a sustainable long-term financial strategy.

Being clear about how much is needed – for capital expenditure and working capital – is essential. Minimising purchases of equipment reduces funds tied up in fixed assets and cash remains free to provide the life-blood of a business ie working capital – the money pumping through the bank account to enable essential everyday payments to be made. If this working capital is insufficient, the business could collapse despite having profitable projects in the pipeline.

Three Ways to Count Money

Three financial windows

The three ways of looking at the finances of any enterprise are through **three financial windows**, the Income and Expenditure Account, the Balance Sheet and the Cash Flow. Each of these can be reports of past activity or projections anticipating a future situation. Each tells its own story and helps to plan a successful future: the creative entrepreneur needs to understand and use all three.

The **Income and Expenditure Account**[17] shows the profit made over a particular period, usually one year. (Even for not-for-profit organisations this is a crucial concept. The co-operative movement prefers the word 'surplus' and this term can be substituted throughout the rest of this chapter if required.)

> *turnover is vanity but profit is sanity*

The **Balance Sheet** shows the total value (net worth) of a business at a particular point in time. It's a 'snapshot' of the assets, liabilities and equity of the owners. The balance sheet indicates the financial strength and capabilities of a business.

The **Cash Flow Report** shows where cash came from and went to in the past. Crucially, a cash flow projection indicates when cash is likely to come and go in the future, on a monthly or weekly basis in the foreseeable future. A cash flow projection is a vital tool of financial management.

Financial accounts are the reports for legal and tax purposes and tend to be produced long after the event. In contrast, management accounts are for managers to use in real time. It is the information you need, when and how you need it, to enable you to keep an eye on what's happening and guide the business through good and bad times.

Cash Flow – or lack of it – is the quickest killer so the management of cash flow must be of most immediate concern in day-to-day management. As long as cash flow is healthy then rises or falls in profitability can be survived, though unprofitable activities will hit cash flow sooner or later.

It's vital to manage the cash flow but essential also to understand the profitability that creates cash. An effective business person knows the profitability of each project in the enterprise, not just their combined total.

Each project or department needs to make a contribution to the overheads of the organisation as well as cover its own direct costs. Or to put it another way, a proportion of core costs need to be allocated to each project or department.

The balance sheet shows the value of the business at specific points, past, present and future. This is public information for a limited company and gives outsiders a statement of the net worth of a company in terms of fixed assets (equipment and property), current assets (cash and bills receivable), and current liabilities (overdrafts and bills payable). It is against these assets that the company might want to borrow funds.

Many creative and cultural enterprises focus on sales (turnover) instead of profit. As they say, "turnover is vanity but profit is sanity". Even for social enterprises where profit is not the prime concern, losses can be fatal. Clearly, profit is derived from the difference between income and expenditure so the control of costs is essential too.

Controlling Costs

There are two kinds of costs to control. Firstly **variable costs** (the costs that will go up and down depending on the level of sales), because reducing variable costs will help make activities and projects more profitable.

Secondly controlling **fixed costs** (the costs you are committed to paying whether you're busy or not) will help avoid cash flow problems and potential disaster during the leaner times. Low fixed costs also enable you to be less dependent on constantly high sales and so less desperate to bring in cash at any cost – for example having to do unprofitable projects for non-target customers – see Mando Group. Use your cash flow forecast to see how soon a cash crisis could occur if business hits a temporary downturn with different fixed cost scenarios. Being able to survive the bad times sometimes amounts to having a philosophy of keeping fixed costs as low as possible.

Ideas in Action — see page 94

One of the biggest costs is staff time and so this needs to be monitored to get useful management information, control costs and increase profitability. Romanian branding company Grapefruit uses an automated system to record staff time spent on projects, good practice learnt in the USA by the company's Chief Creative Officer, Marius Ursache.

Raising Funds

Raising funds is essentially a job of persuading investors that they will get a return on their investment.

This applies whether it's a bank that needs to know how you will be able to repay the capital and interest, or a shareholder who needs to predict a return on investment from profits and dividends. A public funding agency will need to be assured of your long-term survival so as to maintain 'public benefit' in order to justify their investment from the public purse. (Financial viability may include match-funding from other sources or a degree of self-generated income.)

So whichever way you are looking for funds, the starting point is not the application form but the creation of a feasible business formula, in other words a sustainable 'business model', which will provide predictable financial results. It is essential to get the business formula right in the first place before writing it up into a business plan. Mando Group obtained a number of loans on the basis of its business plan, as did JAB Design.

Ideas in Action
— see pages 94 & 70

Predictions involve risk and the degree of predictability depends on the investor's attitude to risk. Investors are often risk-averse and will require a charge on your assets. Intangible assets such as intellectual property are notoriously difficult to use as security. Banks will insist that the risk is partly yours by taking guarantees based on your business assets or personal property, whereas venture capital firms will generally accept more risk but expect a greater payback in terms of a large slice of your business.

There are numerous schemes to provide start-up grants or loans for specific types of business in particular regions. They change so frequently that it is not worth being specific here. Seek financial advice from professionals, mentors, friends and support agencies to apply to loan guarantee schemes, to take advantage of tax breaks or to obtain partnership funding. It's worth noting that as well as collecting taxes, HM Revenue and Customs also provide extensive help and advice. Business support agencies will have up-to-date advice and their contact details can be found on the website *(see the Further Information section at the end of the book)*.

It should be noted that there are always conditions attached to grants and loans and the application process can take time and possibly delay projects. In the worst cases I have seen inappropriate grant aid push organisations in the wrong direction. Sometimes businesses ask for help to get grants and loans when what they really need is a different business model to make them stronger and less dependent on grants or loans. It is therefore advisable to assess the disadvantages as well as the advantages of grants and loans before deciding whether or not to apply for them.

Your Financial Control Panel

Finance and accounting are often regarded as the boring side of business by creative people, but those who ignore it are not in control of their business destiny. It's like driving a car without looking at the dashboard. Successful entrepreneurs don't need to look at all the detailed financial information but do need sight of the key financial measures. These are the equivalent of the car's dashboard instruments showing the

'keep an eye on the profitability and cash flow dials'

Financial Dashboard

Business Dashboard
see page 99

important information such as speed, fuel and oil pressure. The financial equivalents are profitability (per project and overall), cash flow and net assets.

What each enterprise needs is a simple but effective **Financial Dashboard**, constantly visible when driving the business. More sophisticated measures include financial trends and ratios. Unless you have one eye on the profitability and cash flow dials, you're heading for a crash – or an empty tank in the fast lane!

A more comprehensive **Business Dashboard** will take into account other vital indicators as well as the main financial measures.

Creating Financial Security

Financial security is derived from creating income streams that are not dependent on your continuous labour. These are the income streams that flow while you sleep. The things that create this cash flow can also be sold at a later date. In the creative industries, this is most obviously achieved through the utilisation or exploitation of your intellectual property. Intellectual property rights, managed skilfully, enable a creator to receive ongoing income from a variety of sources. *See Chapter 6: Protecting Your Creativity.*

In a nutshell, the business of creativity is the art of turning creative talent into intellectual property that provides income streams for the owners of that IP.

Key Points

1   Don't wait for the day you have an ideal amount of money – it might never come.

2   Understand your business finances by looking at them from three different perspectives.

3   Use management accounts to monitor and plan your business, not just financial accounts to report on past events.

4   Keep fixed costs under control.

5   To raise funds you will need to show how your business formula will create sustainable income streams.

6   Decide what needs to be measured, then devise a financial dashboard so you can stay in control. Keep one eye on the dials so that you don't crash – or run out of fuel in the fast lane.

7   Get expert advice on taxation, VAT etc from an accountant.

8   It's not just about business profits – social enterprises need to generate surpluses too.

9   Be aware of the strings attached to grants and loans.

10   Create financial security through the exploitation of your Intellectual Property.

Ideas in Action

JAB Design Consultancy
Industrial Product Design

JAB Design is an international award-winning product design company which works with innovators and manufacturers to develop commercially-successful new products. The company has experience in designing medical devices, lighting, furniture, laboratory automation, consumables, electronics enclosures and several other types of product.

Managing Director Jonathan Butters says: "Instead of specialising in just one field we work across conventional specialisms because it's the interface between them that's interesting and creative. For example we design medical equipment, traditionally used only by specialists, for use by patients in their own homes using our expertise of designing consumer goods. Similarly, the interface between psychology and engineering, or electronics and sociology also gives rise to creative new designs."

"Good design cannot be the ego-centric creation of the designer working alone. Design is a process," he emphasises. "The design process involves a dialogue with the client to address the needs of various communities of interest including the end user and those responsible for the product's sale, maintenance and disposal." Good designers can deal with customers' needs and he points out that creative geniuses such as Caravaggio and Da Vinci worked mainly for customers, rather than in artistic isolation and were still able to put some of themselves into their creations without any contradiction between artistic integrity and clients' requirements.

With a background in engineering, Jonathan started in business as a sole trader in 1999 and in 2001 devised a business growth strategy for a new company with the help of business support agencies including Creative Business Solutions. Their business plan identified growth areas to focus on, such as biotechnology, medical and safety equipment amongst others. In each area they have designed successful products which led to more work in that field. It's a growth technique Jonathan describes as "using a small fish to catch a bigger fish".

Business growth depended on loans and Jonathan found to his dismay (this was no surprise!) that banks and other funders were "on the whole a risk-averse bunch". His own bank turned down his application for a loan and other institutions were equally reluctant at first. It wasn't until he put his own money where his mouth was, by re-mortgaging his own home, that he was able to find funders willing to share the risk. "Funders want to know that you're going to feel the pain of the challenge and put your all into making the business work." The final funding package of around £200K was made up from loans from the Merseyside Special Investment Fund, the Small Firms Guarantee Scheme (through Lloyds TSB) plus re-mortgaging his own home. There was also grant money from Business Link and BusinessLiverpool.

Since then, JAB Design has grown into a thriving business with 9 staff, 20 clients and a turnover of around £750k per annum. Before employing

staff Jonathan invested in legal advice to ensure the company's contract of employment was comprehensive. Since then the company has been able to deal with some staff issues following the correct procedures without opening themselves up to appeals and counterclaims, due to having up-to-date contracts of employment.

No longer a one-man band, Jonathan now spends more time working on the business rather than in it, what he calls "occupying higher ground". His staff concentrate on design work using high-end technology – SolidWorks 3D CAD software and he supervises all projects "adding a qualitative layer over the top" as he puts it. One of his key tasks is liaising with customers, which includes writing the briefs and technical specifications, agreeing stages of work with the client and managing customers' expectations, all of which call for "United Nations level diplomacy at times" according to Jonathan.

The company's Terms of Trade (available on its website) were established early on with specialist input and Jonathan looks back at this as an important move. They have been amended twice since then, to clarify some issues raised by particular clients. JAB Design have since had a significant dispute with a client and managed to gain a settlement out of court because of the robust nature of their terms and conditions of trade.

Important clauses deal with the assignment of intellectual property to the client. Crucially, this release of IP is tied to client payments, thereby safeguarding cash flow. In recent developments, JAB Design has negotiated payments through royalties on product sales in exchange for a reduction in design fees.

Talking about the company's values, Jonathan says "we are enthusiastic about products that increase quality of life, not trivial stuff. Medical and safety equipment is important to us and quality of life includes sports and leisure products. We don't do military work." Another JAB Design project, a new safety product for the deep-sea fishing industry which is predicted to save 50 lives a year, was still subject to client confidentiality at the time of writing. Watch this space!

8

Keeping Good Company

— This chapter explains limited and unlimited financial liability and the pros and cons of setting up a limited company for your business as well as considering other corporate structures.
— Different organisational structures are outlined as well as concepts such as the 'virtual organisation'.

The vast majority of businesses employ less than ten people and the creative industries are no exception – many are one-person enterprises, operating on a self-employed basis as sole traders. Other creative businesses have set up as companies or social enterprises.

Financial Liability

Whilst self-employment has some benefits it also has disadvantages, including **unlimited liability** for the owner since in legal terms the business and the individual are one and the same thing. The owner's personal and business finances are all in one 'pot'. This unlimited liability also applies to partnerships (except in the case of a Limited Liability Partnership).

Limited liability is usually achieved through setting up a 'limited' company as a separate entity or vehicle for the business so that the liability of the investors (members) is limited to the amount they have chosen to invest in it. If the business goes bust, their losses are limited to their business investment, not their personal possessions. (This contrasts with 'unlimited liability' sole traders and partners who might have to pay off business debts with personal funds.)

Even with a limited company, a bank may require personal guarantees against a business loan if the business does not have sufficient suitable assets. The liability is then effectively transferred away from the company to the person guaranteeing the loan.

It's important that everyone involved in the enterprise understands their financial liability.

‘
understand your financial liability
’

Limited Companies

Setting up a private limited company is straightforward and the pros and cons should be considered.

In law, a limited company is regarded as a separate legal 'person'. This separation is an essential element of providing limited liability for its members. It also means that it is the company that owns the assets – and can be sued in a court of law – not the individual shareholders.

One of several considerations for smaller enterprises is the 'image' of having limited company status, which may give the business more credibility than sole trader status, depending on the sector you are in, and customers' perceptions.

A company with shares provides a useful device for fundraising by issuing shares in the business to investors and bringing in other people as the business grows, either as shareholders, directors or both.

One of the disadvantages of companies is that they must submit details of directors and annual accounts to Companies House, where this information is made available for public inspection.

Social Enterprises

The benefits of limited liability also apply to not-for-profit organisations (or more precisely, non-profit-distributing organisations). These can register as a 'company limited by guarantee without share capital', which is a company just like any other but with no shares and therefore unable to distribute profits as dividends to shareholders. Companies of this kind can also become Registered Charities. A social enterprise – a business with primarily social aims – will usually register a company although some co-operatives are Industrial and Provident Societies. The new **Community Interest Company** status can be applied to companies with or without shares and has been introduced to provide a specific legal status for social enterprises.

Community Interest Company

Depending on the range of business activity you are involved in and taking into account partnership working with other individuals and businesses, there may be a case for using more than one structure for your business activities.

As companies grow, they may acquire other businesses, give birth to subsidiaries, or split into separate legal entities if new opportunities with different business strategies require alternative structures. Charities often set up a separate company as a trading subsidiary. Businesses set up separate companies for the sake of image and branding, ownership and involvement, sale of intellectual property or reduction of overall risk. See The Windows Project and New Mind.

Ideas in Action — see pages 102 & 42

Organisational Structures

To work effectively in the project-based environment, organisations need to take on new forms. The traditional steady-state company with a fixed number of employees and a traditional hierarchical structure is not suited to this new environment. The information-age enterprises need new organisational structures, which have been called: Virtual, Network, Shamrock and Club Sandwich organisations.

Such organisational models are not special legal structures but concepts about flexible ways of organising business activities.

Virtual Organisation

A **Virtual Organisation** can be 'invisible' insofar as there is no identifiable headquarters; its members might be geographically remote and probably connected through the Internet. Virtual organisations can form quickly for a particular purpose from a number of individuals and organisations in a network. Often the majority of its work is subcontracted to associate companies. The virtual organisation co-ordinates this work and controls the intellectual capital and other intangibles such as branding. The virtual organisation can disappear as soon as the job is done, yet its individual members can rapidly reform in a different combination giving rise to a new virtual organisation.

A **Network Organisation** can describe several separate organisations or individuals working together for a common goal, for example a designer, manufacturer and suppliers. The term can also be used to describe a larger organisation in which the various parts inter-react in a more organic and autonomous way than in a traditional hierarchical structure.

A **Shamrock Organisation** is Charles Handy's[18] name for a business of three parts – the core staff, freelance project workers and subcontracted firms. Red Production Company is a good example of this model. With a small core staff, it engages hundreds of freelance workers needed for TV drama productions and it outsources functions such as merchandising to a separate joint-venture enterprise.

Ideas in Action — see page 78

Club Sandwich Organisation

Building on the shamrock model is my concept of the **Club Sandwich Organisation** which:

A. acknowledges creative individuals who need the social interaction and facilities of a 'members club',
B. provides a metaphor for the three 'layers' of core staff, freelance workers and subcontracted firms, and also
C. the different relationships and levels of bonding between the three slices which can be likened to the different fillings of a Club Sandwich.

Thinking through matters of corporate structures may seem like unnecessary hassle in the early days of a creative enterprise, but getting this part of the business formula right can prevent a lot of headaches later on and help you along your road to success.

In conclusion, decisions about organisational structures should support your business strategy, not drive it.

Key Points

1   Understand your financial liability.

2   Consider the pros and cons of setting up a company to limit your financial liability.

3   Consider having separate companies for different activities and projects to compartmentalise business risk.

4   Be clear about where you are going. Do you want a lifestyle business or an enterprise you can eventually sell? Use different structures to support your business strategy – don't let your structure dictate your business direction.

5   Social enterprises should consider the Community Interest Company option.

6   Getting the corporate structure right early on could save lots of hassle later.

7   Look at your structure from an image and branding point of view – the customers' perspective.

8   Take specialist advice as required from a business adviser or accountant.

9   Consider partnerships through virtual organisations.

10 Decide which aspects of your enterprise should be handled in-house or subcontracted.

Ideas in Action

Red Production Company
TV Drama Production Company

Clocking Off, *The Second Coming* and *Casanova* are some of the TV dramas produced by the award-winning Red Production Company. *Queer as Folk*, written by Russell T Davies was its first success after Red was founded by Nicola Shindler, who already had a fine track record with productions such as *Hillsborough* written by Jimmy McGovern.

"TV production is a freelance world," says managing director Andrew Critchley, and so Red engages freelance staff to expand and contract according to its productions' needs. With a core of just 8 employees, and renting an office within another TV company, Red keeps its fixed costs to the minimum. A classic 'project organisation', Red can engage several hundred people on a freelance basis as needed for its various productions.

A successful enterprise in both artistic and commercial terms, Red's profitability is derived mainly from its scale rather than its profit margins, according to Andrew Critchley. A £5m production with just 5% margin still represents a significant £0.25m profit.

Red sets up limited companies for each production and these 'single purpose vehicles' (SPVs) enable Red to divide the business risks associated with each venture into separate compartments. Red Production Company Ltd is at the centre of a number of other associated companies, such as Second Coming Ltd, Linda Green Ltd, Bob and Rose Ltd, each company an SPV for its associated production. The whole business of each production is put through its own company and the SPVs continue to be active in order to collect ongoing income streams from the sale of rights, format fees and DVDs for their respective productions.

Changes in the business environment for TV production has seen the terms of trade shift in favour of independent producers who now retain a greater percentage of intellectual property rights in their productions. This has come about due to the intervention of Pact[19] and changes in Ofcom regulations.[20] Responding to this change and taking advantage of new opportunities, Red increasingly exploits the intellectual property in its productions through the sale of rights, format fees (such as the sale of the format of *Queer as Folk* to a US cable network) and DVDs of its TV series.

This marketing and merchandising has been achieved through the DVD label 'inD', a joint venture with production companies from different genres to form inD DVD Ltd.

www.redproductioncompany.com
www.ind-dvd.co.uk

Red Productions *Mine All Mine* (top) and *Casanova*

Links to related ideas and topics in book:
* **Separate Company Structures** (see pg 75)
* **Changes in the external environment (Regulations)** (see pg 28)
* **Low fixed costs** (see pg 65 – 66)
* **Virtual Organisations** (see pg 75)
* **Exploitation of Intellectual Property via merchandising** (see pg 58)

9

Leadership and Management

— This section looks at the change from working 'in' your business to working 'on' your business.
— It explores managing and leading people, both employees and others, using different leadership styles and dealing with change through leadership.
— It also looks at some aspects of employing people.

Management can be defined as 'the achievement of aims through other people' and the job of a manager therefore is to co-ordinate the activities of other people to get things done. For many people, the transition from 'doing it yourself' to managing others is a difficult one and this often applies to creative people who set up their one-person business and then employ other people as the enterprise grows.

The manager's job as co-ordinator can be compared to that of an air traffic controller whose job is to make sure that planes come and go safely, without collisions. Their job is not to fly planes themselves. The frustration of being a manager is that you no longer fly planes because your job is now to co-ordinate others' work to help them to do it well.

Working 'in' and 'on' the business

In most organisations, as people are promoted they tend to become more removed from the original job that attracted them in the first place and this applies to teachers, salespeople, nurses and others. It's the same for creative entrepreneurs, who often tell me that as their business grows they have less time for creative endeavour directly and spend more time on administration and managing other people. Perhaps that's one reason why many business people do not aim for business growth in terms of employing lots of people but want to build lifestyle businesses instead. Most people set up in business because they want to create a job for themselves working **in** the business, but it's essential for an entrepreneur who wants to grow their enterprise to focus on working **on** the business. The captain of a ship needs to navigate from the bridge, not work in the engine room. If you want to build a business that you can eventually sell, you must construct it so that eventually you are not involved at all. It's important to be clear about your aims and objectives.

'are you working in or on the business?'

the effective leader needs to use different leadership styles

Leadership Styles

Getting things done through other people can be difficult for a number of reasons. At first it takes longer to train someone else than to do it yourself. The level of communication needed to make them fully aware of everything you know about the business is immense. Taking on the first administrator, for example, frees you of some paperwork but at the same time ties you into being a manager. Communication within a team is essential but can be extremely time-consuming. As the number of people in the business grows, the communication required between them expands exponentially. Deciding what people do and don't need to know, how they get to know, and who tells them, is a management job in itself.

Leadership

The word leadership often brings to mind some of the world's great leaders of nations and movements: Nelson Mandela, Winston Churchill, Mahatma Ghandi, Martin Luther King, etc and so it can seem much too grand a term for the boss of a five-person design firm. However, the requirements for leadership (as opposed to management) are still the same. Broadly speaking, management concentrates on telling people what to do, whereas leadership focuses on telling people where they are going, then inspiring them and enabling them to play their part in the journey.

The effective leader needs to know different **Leadership Styles** – and ideally to be fluent in all the 'languages' of leadership, using each of them appropriately at different times according to circumstances. My own terms for the leadership styles based on those suggested by Daniel Goleman[21] are:

Dictator — the macho boss
Visionary — inspires with a vision
People-person — personable, communicator
Listener — consultative, democratic
Superman/woman — sets a fast pace of work
Nurturer — coaches and develops others

The trick is to be able to use all of the leadership styles – and know when it is appropriate to do so.

Just as it is often jokingly said that the business is ok but for its customers, leadership and management would be easy if they didn't involve dealing with people. People come in all shapes and sizes: employees, partners, customers, associates, suppliers etc and can at times be awkward, demanding, overenthusiastic, distracted, talkative, stubborn or just downright irrational!

Emotional Intelligence

To work well with people, it's essential to have a good measure of **Emotional Intelligence** which I define as 'an ability to manage ourselves and our relationships with other people effectively, by understanding our own and other people's feelings, recognising that we human beings have an emotional as well as a rational side to our make-up.'

It's no coincidence that the people who rise to become leaders of their businesses or institutions are those who have skills of communication and emotional intelligence as well as a creative, academic or technical speciality.

There are different types of leadership – it doesn't have to be about the charismatic macho stereotype. Some of the best leaders are personally modest whilst being also ruthlessly ambitious for their companies – what's been called the **Level 5 Leader**.[22]

Level 5 Leader

Inspirational leaders provide what most employees say they want from their bosses – inspiration – though only 11% say they actually get it, according to a survey undertaken in the UK by the Department for Trade and Industry.[23]

Lateral thinking leaders search for and listen to ideas from outside their own industry or culture to find great ideas or new techniques, then apply them imaginatively to their own enterprise. So this lateral thinking leadership in the creative industries would acknowledge ideas from outside the creative sector, and then apply creativity to using those ideas within it.

Managing Change

The 'management of change' is a perennial business topic since change itself is constant. But the management of change is to some extent a misnomer. I prefer the term 'leading change' because, importantly, change needs leadership as much as management and 'change management' tends to imply that change is an administrative or technical job. In reality it's more about inspiring people towards a vision and giving them the freedom and support to do what's needed to get there.

Employing People

Leading and managing people certainly applies to employees, but employing staff is not the only way to grow a business – or to lead people.

Ideas in Action — see page 24

what most people want from their boss is inspiration

The pros and cons of employing people versus engaging freelancers needs to be considered carefully and some organisations use a powerful blend of both. **Peppered Sprout** is an example of a business which uses both contracted permanent employees combined with a database of freelance artists. Network businesses and virtual organisations are prevalent in the creative sector – *see Chapter 8: Keeping Good Company* for more ideas about structures.

The benefits of employing people are mainly in having constant and exclusive access to their time and expertise – and ownership of their creative output *(see Chapter 6: Protecting your Creativity)*. On the negative side, there is the commitment to the fixed costs of salaries and the legal responsibilities of being an employer.

Freelancers can provide the skills you need, just when you need them without the fixed costs, though the hourly rate will be higher. The responsibility is less, but so is the control – of their time, availability and creativity.

The big step from being a one-person operation to taking on your first member of staff is a crucial one and marks a turning point from working **in** the business to working **on** the business.

Ideas in Action — see page 70

JAB Design took legal advice about their contract of employment (as well as their terms of trade) at a very early stage. Keeping abreast of employment regulations, taxation and benefits, as well as operating good systems and procedures for induction, training appraisals, staff development, remuneration, grievances and disciplinary matters is just one more aspect of managing people within a successful creative enterprise.

Key Points

1   Are you prepared to become an 'air traffic controller'?

2   To what extent do you work 'in' or 'on' the business?

3   Be a leader as well as a manager.

4   Are your employees some of the 11% who are inspired by their leader?

5   Are you a lateral thinking leader who learns from other industries then adapts their ideas?

6   Build in time for communication with your staff and between members of the staff team.

7   Learn – and use – the six different leadership styles.

8   Develop your emotional intelligence to be able to work with people even better.

9   Weigh up the pros and cons of employing people versus using freelancers.

10   Ensure your employment contracts and procedures are watertight and up to date.

Ideas in Action

The Team
Brand Communication Consultancy

The Team is ranked as the most effective brand communication consultancy in the UK by *Design Week* surveys 2002, 2003 and 2004. The company boasts an impressive array of clients from the private, public and not-for-profit sectors, including Vodafone, the NHS, Comic Relief, the BBC, the Chartered Institute of Personnel and Development, the Beatles and the Metropolitan Police.

Managing Director Julian Grice was one of the four designers who started The Team 20 years ago. "In those days it was really four separate businesses, with each designer adopting a different business model, dealing with different clients and focusing on different types of work," says Julian.

Eight years ago, The Team assessed its internal strengths and weaknesses and came to the conclusion that they were "leaderless". As a result, The Team redesigned its business and now has "a second generation management team with a carefully chosen mix of skills and experience. Eight people, each with a different voice," as Julian describes it.

The Team's success is a result of a deliberate integration of creativity and business. Julian's role as leader includes "carefully crafting an atmosphere where people's views are respected, whether they are in 'creative' or 'business' roles," he says. The Team is then able to bring together its various skills to focus on clients' needs. "We enjoy achieving things for clients," he adds.

In a sector that Julian believes is generally not good at managing customer relationships, The Team pride themselves on being "hugely pragmatic, applying creative thinking to real life situations." "Creativity is not on the Board agenda," he says, "because it's assumed to be in everything we do." Everything at The Team takes place in the context of clients' needs and they focus on particular market niches.

The Team moved consciously towards public sector clients in the late 1990s. This was partly because they found that their passion for communicating issues produced their best work in this sector and partly to avoid the economic cycle which affects the private sector. As the company has grown and invested in skills and systems, this move into the public sector has become more focused.

The Team is clear about its strategy, who its clients are and significantly, what it will not do. The company has a policy of 'saying no' to potential customers in the tobacco, defence and property development industries for ethical reasons. For more practical reasons, they will not take on projects if the company does not have a technical specialisation, such as in retailing or packaging. Risk Analysis is a factor too and The Team will decline business to avoid the business risk associated with some particular clients and projects.

In the area of personnel development, The Team again blends principles and pragmatism. To increase staff commitments and reduce staff turnover The Team has worked closely with the Chartered Institute of Personnel and Development (CIPD) to adopt best practices in human resource management. Every member of staff has a Personal Development Portfolio or PDP which, importantly, is driven by the employee, not the management. "We take the view that everything is a learning opportunity," says Julian, to describe their 'learning organisation', mentioning a range of means 'by which people learn at work, adding that ironically, formal training is often the least effective of these.

Julian Grice

The Team recruits staff from design colleges with which they have close links through key tutors. By providing placement opportunities for students, the company can assess potential employees, both in terms of their creativity and crucially in their ability to work pragmatically for clients – another example of The Team's effectiveness in blending creative and business thinking.

Links to related ideas and topics in book:
* **Blending creativity and business effectively** (see pg 8)
* **Evaluating strengths and weaknesses** (see pg 17)
* **Market Segmentation** (see pg 37)
* **Focusing on clients' needs** (see pg 36)
* **Leadership** (see pg 82)
* **Saying No** (see pg 92)
* **Risk Analysis** (see pg 100)
* **Continuing Professional Development** (see pg 21)
* **Personal Development Portfolios** (see pg 21)
* **Learning Organisations** (see pg 22)

10
Business Feasibility

— This chapter gives you an opportunity – and a specific technique – to test the feasibility of your business ideas so that you can choose those that will give you a feasible formula for your creative business.

it's fatal to assume that creativity 'deserves' business success

Saying No
see page 92

 **Feasibility Filter**

You have your creativity and your goals, but these alone are not enough. You need a feasible business formula – or else you could fail like so many other creative, intelligent and enthusiastic people have done before you.

It's fatal to assume that any creativity can be turned into a successful business, or to believe that wonderful creativity 'deserves' business success. It takes more than just any old mix of brilliant creativity and a bunch of potential customers to make a successful formula that achieves the desired financial result. The knack is to be able to recognise which formulae are likely to succeed or fail – and to do this quickly and painlessly before precious time, energy and money are wasted.

This requires having more than one rigid idea and a method of selecting those which are feasible, then choosing the best one from all the good ones. Since we are capable of creating more than one idea, judging one particular idea to be not feasible is not a 'failure', but simply one more step along the road to success. The job to be done by entrepreneurs and those who want to help them is not to take the first idea you thought of and somehow make it work by throwing money, marketing advice or training at it. It's also about **Saying No** to those ideas which are not likely to be feasible.

What's needed is a method for examining ideas to find out whether (or not) each idea is feasible in order to select the one or two that are most likely to succeed. We need to generate lots of ideas and then have a method to select the best. I use a technique for assessing the feasibility of creative enterprises which I call the **Feasibility Filter.**[24]

The Feasibility Filter

It provides a way of assessing the best bright ideas, projects and business opportunities in two ways simultaneously:

Does it use our creativity to the full and allow it to shine?

Is there a market which we can work with profitably to provide sustainable income streams ?

Clearly these questions need to be answered in the context of your Values.

This **Feasibility Filter** should be applied to each product, service or project you are considering to find those which score highest against both questions.

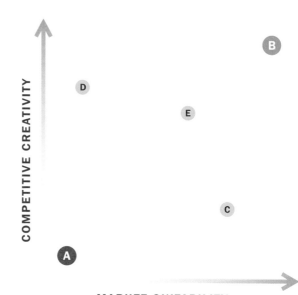

COMPETITIVE CREATIVITY
is the degree to which you can solve clients' problems better than your competitors can.

MARKET SUITABILITY
is the degree to which specific clients and market segments can help you achieve your financial objectives.

The diagram is illustrated with two contrasting examples:

(A) Is a product or service where your creativity is less able to provide a customer benefit than your competitors AND where the market segment does not supply sufficient net income.

(B) Is a product or service which uses your creativity to produce customer benefits better than your competitors AND the customers in sufficient number are able and willing to pay the price you require.

For example a web design company may have a range of skills and several possible markets.

One idea might be to design websites for schools, but the Feasibility Filter highlights the fact that there are competitors who are better at serving this market and the reality that schools do not have the budgets to make the work financially viable. (This is represented by **(A)** in the diagram.)

On the other hand, an option to work for government agencies could show up as an area where there is a competitive advantage and a financially lucrative market segment. (This is illustrated by **(B)** in the diagram.)

Many other positions on the filter are possible and these are shown as **(C) (D)** and **(E)**.

Business Formula
see page 97

By plotting several different ideas on the Feasibility Filter, we can choose those that will produce the most feasible elements for your **Business Formula**. By using the Feasibility Filter, in combination with creating new ideas, you can combine business know-how with creativity to find a viable formula for success more quickly.

Ideas in Action — see page 102

Mission and Values
see page 11

be prepared to say no

Saying No

I have used the Feasibility Filter approach to help many creative businesses. It can also be applied to not-for-profit organisations. **The Windows Project** used a method based on this approach to select opportunities which combine its creative skills and financial viability in the context of its specific **Mission** and **Values**.

If a proposal doesn't hold together to form a workable business formula, maybe it needs to be amended – or taken right back to the drawing board.

And that's ok! It's better to revise your proposal and get it right than to rush in and fail. And as creative people we can think of plenty of other ideas if the first few just don't add up to a feasible formula.

The other chapters of this book will help you devise and revise your ideas taking into account changing conditions, customers' needs, competitive forces, and other aspects of business. Then use the Feasibility Filter to test and revise them until the best ones emerge.

"No!"

Saying No[25] to unfeasible or unstrategic projects should be regarded as a strength not a weakness.

Timothy Chan, Chinese computer games entrepreneur and one of the richest men in China, models himself on Bill Gates in this respect, saying that Gates is so great because he can resist temptation.[26] Both have enough money to venture into other industries, yet they have the strategic self-discipline not to diversify.

Key Points

1 Creative talent does not automatically 'deserve' business success.

2 Business feasibility is a matter of finding a business formula that matches specific aspects of your creativity with specific customers' needs.

3 What creativity do you have that can satisfy specific customers' needs better than your competitors?

4 Which specific market segments can provide you with suitable income streams?

5 Use the Feasibility Filter to assess different options for business ideas, projects, products, services and market segments.

6 The Feasibility Filter works for not-for-profit organisations too.

7 It's better to test ideas against the Feasibility Filter and find that they may not work than to test them in real life with the possible loss of morale, money, time and other resources.

8 Be prepared to reformulate your ideas to make them feasible.

9 Refer back to different chapters of this book when re-thinking your ideas.

10 As you test the feasibility of different options, remain true to your creative passion and values.

Ideas in Action

Mando Group
Web Development and Design Consultancy

'Mando Group is a web development and design consultancy. We're here to help our clients become more successful.'

"That's our mission statement," says Mando Group Managing Director Matt Johnson, "but it took a lot of iterations over 5 years to make it so concise and accurate." The Mando Group are clear about what they do – and what they don't do. Web development is 80% of their business and the other 20% is from design work. The company doesn't undertake projects that are outside this brief.

Matt and business partner Ian Finch have built a corporate culture based on their Values. Creativity, Openness, Responsive and Engaging are the four values that underpin the way they do business and they recruit only people who can embrace those values.

The business was set up by three students in 1997 using their student loans as capital and traded under the name 'Web Shed' until 2002. With assistance from Merseyside ACME and loans from various sources, the company was debt financed to the tune of £250K at one point as the directors invested heavily in business development to achieve the company's growth ambitions.

Mando have a "passion to deliver" and can be "aggressively focused" on winning business says Matt. Early contracts with Mersey TV's *Brookside* and *Hollyoaks* opened doors to other clients including the international computer games giant Capcom.

The Group focuses almost exclusively on the public sector and larger SMEs, saying 'No' to potential customers who don't fit the profile of clients that they can best serve profitably. This profile is based on the size of the company, location and credit ratings amongst other factors. Matt admits that in the early days they were "not gutsy enough" to turn down business because they were desperate for cash and ended up dealing with "nightmare customers" who turned out to be more expensive than if they had simply borrowed the money they needed at the time.

Mando uses Key Performance Indicators (KPIs) to measure business performance on a weekly and monthly basis. These KPIs include metrics such as sales, new leads found and acted on, proposals sent to clients, cash received, billing predictions and debtor analysis as well as profitability. This data is used daily for management information purposes and forms the basis for reports to the Board.

These KPIs form a business dashboard that Matt watches as he drives the business successfully towards its growth targets.

www.mandogroup.com

Consumer website for Capcom Europe

Links to related ideas and topics in book:
* **Mission** (see pg 11)
* **Values** (see pg 11)
* **Key Performance Indicators** (see pg 99)
* **Loans** (see pg 66)
* **Focus on market segments** (see pg 37)
* **Saying No** (see pg 92)

11
Your Route to Success

— This chapter is concerned with pulling together all the elements considered so far and formulating a specific plan for your feasible creative business.

Vision
see page 11

Business Strategy

Business Formula

SWOT Analysis

Firstly you need to be clear about the success you want to achieve – your **Vision**.

Then you need a realistic plan to get there – your **Business Strategy** or route to success. This route must be based on your unique Business Formula.

A **Business Formula** is your unique mixture of particular products/services at which you excel, carefully selected customers or market segments, which can combine to produce the desired financial result, consistent with your Values.

A feasible business formula must be based on a realistic assessment of the market, competitors and a **SWOT Analysis** of your own Strengths and Weaknesses, combined with Opportunities and Threats in the changing world.

Clearly, you will play to your strengths, seize opportunities, fully understand selected customers' needs and position yourself shrewdly among competitors.

Seven Steps to Success

It can all be boiled down to seven simple steps:

1. **Be clear where you want to go – your Vision.**
2. **Know yourself and your current situation.**
3. **Understand customers' needs, competition and external forces.**
4. **Carefully create your unique Business Formula.**
5. **Devise a plan of action – your Business Strategy.**
6. **Turn the plan into action.**
7. **Stick to it – be prepared to Say No.**

Of course there will be thousands of things to do along the way (tasks) and some important decisions to be made (tactics) but the strategy is about the big issues – the essential milestones or key turning points along the way. It is impossible to plan precisely the exact and detailed series of tasks, or predict the tactics you will have to use, but there will be several essential big steps to be taken. These will be different for each enterprise but they might include vital matters such as finding an international partner, investing in new technology, protecting and exploiting intellectual property, attracting investment, etc.

A creative way to think about this is to imagine you are in the future and have achieved your success. In an interview, telling the story of your journey, you look back on the key decisions and actions that proved to be turning points or vital ingredients of your success. Perhaps there were four or five critical moves that you will look back on from the future. Returning to the present, you now have a list of the key things you need to do.

Note that this applies equally to not-for-profit organisations as well as commercial businesses and can be applied to personal as well as organisational goals.

Implementing a strategy is not always easy to plan since you cannot predict just how and when particular opportunities will arise or circumstances change, but if you know what you are looking for, you can look in the right direction, or spot opportunities if they come your way.

A vital ingredient of implementing the plan is sticking to it and that means **Saying No** to opportunities that are not in line with your business formula and strategic plan.

'be clear where you want to get to'

Saying No
see page 92

Measuring Performance

Along the way, you will need to monitor progress in different ways: firstly to make sure you are not deviating substantially from your business formula and are right on track to hit the key milestones; secondly to make sure that your business is progressing at the right pace. Deciding what needs to improve, and what doesn't, is an integral part of a clear business strategy.

Key Performance Indicators

You can then set targets for improving the important things and these can be called **Key Performance Indicators (KPIs)**. Depending on your business, they might include targets for sales, customer satisfaction, profitability, innovation, growth, market penetration, developing core skills, etc. See Mando Group.

Ideas in Action — see page 94

Using the balanced scorecard[27] approach, these should include financial measures but not exclusively. A **Business Dashboard** for your own enterprise should also take into account customers, creativity, learning, and efficiency. This provides you with a business dashboard or control panel which constantly shows how things are developing and quickly brings to your attention anything that isn't going well so that you can take appropriate action immediately.

Business Dashboard

Imagine you are away from the business for a year, but want to know how things are going. What ten pieces of information would you want to receive on a single piece of paper each week to give you an overview of the business? The answer to this is your specification for designing your own business dashboard.

Triple Bottom Line

Depending on your philosophies and priorities you may want to measure success using the **Triple Bottom Line** approach, measuring financial performance, social benefits and the environmental impact of your business. This is a way that social enterprises measure success and is increasingly being adopted by large corporations who are eager to demonstrate that their motivations are not purely financial.

Risks

Risks are part of any business and calculated risks will have to be taken, based on a Risk Analysis. You will probably face a range of financial and legal risks as well as risks to your brand and personal wellbeing.

Risk Analysis

Risk Analysis is simply the technique of listing all risks and ranking them according to their likelihood of happening and the potential negative impact on the business. The point, of course, is to minimise the risks, focusing first on those risks that score high on both counts and making plans to make them less likely to happen and/or have a lesser impact if they do. A calculated assessment of risks is an important element of choosing the best route to success. An action plan to deal with risks will help to navigate that chosen route without mishaps.

your pocket guide on an exciting journey

Business Plans

A detailed business plan is usually required to explain your intentions to investors and partners. Just as importantly, it should provide a useful guide for internal use by the owners / directors and staff. Some people find that writing a business plan is a nightmare. Others find that the exercise produces a useless document. In both cases the reason is often that the proposed business is not based on the solid foundations of a feasible business formula.

It's essential to establish the fundamentals of **why** you are planning to do it as well as **how** you are planning to do it. Once you are clear about these matters and have the framework of a feasible formula which brings together your skills and your selected customers' needs in a financially sustainable way, then the route to success becomes clear and the rest of the business plan will fall into place relatively easily.

Ideas in Action — see page 102

There is no standard template for a business plan. In fact you don't even have to call it a business plan – **The Windows Project** preferred the term Development Plan. It is simply your way of setting out your plans for yourself and for others in a comprehensive, clear and useful way. It should answer all the questions that a potential partner or investor might ask. The best business plans are those that a creative entrepreneur actually *wants to* refer to often and is updated on a rolling basis as time goes by and circumstances change.

Your business plan describes your route to success. It is your pocket guide on an exciting journey and helps you keep going in the right direction as the adventure unfolds.

Key Points

1   Be clear about your goals – your Vision.

2   Know yourself, your business and all those involved.

3   Identify opportunities and threats using the business radar approach and the ICEDRIPS checklist.

4   Use the Feasibility Filter.

5   Identify the crucial steps that you will look back on as turning points.

6   Analyse risks – then minimise them.

7   Measure your progress by monitoring the important things with your own business dashboard.

8   Be prepared to 'say no' to things which distract you from your plan.

9   Get the fundamentals right and a business plan will be easy to write.

10 Write a business plan (or development plan) for your own use as a pocket guide to the journey ahead.

Ideas in Action

The Windows Project
Community Writing Project

The Windows Project is a not-for-profit organisation with a mission to pioneer projects which enable people to develop their creativity through writing, in all sections of the community.

Founded by Dave Ward and Dave Calder over 25 years ago, it was innovative in running writing workshops in play schemes, youth centres and schools. It has a membership of over 40 writers including the internationally recognised Levi Tafari and acts as an agency between the writers and the community.

Looking ahead, the Windows Project is committed to remaining loyal to its mission whilst seeking exciting new opportunities in a fast-changing world. It will pioneer projects in new areas of the wider community and indeed with online and virtual communities.

The project's success over the years has taken place in changing circumstances and the Windows Project has planned for its future by undertaking an analysis of the external environment using the ICEDRIPS checklist to identify opportunities and threats.

Changes in the way schools are funded, the strict child protection regulations applying to those working with young people, including Criminal Records Bureau checks, the reorganisation of the arts funding system, the national curriculum and school inspections via Ofsted, all present challenges for the Windows Project to deal with. On the other hand there are opportunities for collaboration with Creative Partnerships, Arts Council England, the National Health Service and the City of Liverpool, European Capital of Culture 2008. The Internet also provides increasing opportunities to work with online communities in new ways and further develop international links.

The Windows Project involved all its stakeholders in a systematic process to devise a new Development Plan – the organisation's preferred name for a business plan. This included agreeing a shared vision for the future of the project, an analysis of its own strengths and weaknesses and prioritising its strategic objectives.

The Windows Project is constituted as a registered charity in conjunction with an Association which acts as its trading wing for most of its activities. This combination provides maximum flexibility in terms of obtaining charitable funding and generating earned income from contracts for services. The Association is in practice a social enterprise and broadly meets the criteria to become constituted as a new Community Interest Company. It has a community purpose and is accountable to its stakeholders which include Association members, employees, client organisations, funding partners, trustees and other supporters.

www.windowsproject.demon.co.uk

The Windows Project
DEVELOPMENT PLAN
2005 - 2008

The Windows Project's vision of the future remains true to its core Mission and Values so it will continue to focus on communities, recognising that its strengths and competencies are in this area. The Project will continue to balance its creative and social mission with economic realities by operating a 'mixed economy' of grants and contracts for services. Using a technique based on the principles of the Feasibility Filter, Windows will select projects in future which meet the dual criteria of fulfiling its social mission and ensuring the Project's financial sustainability.

On this basis, the Windows Project is set to stay true to its Values and Mission during changing circumstances and continue to pioneer new projects over the next 25 years.

Links to related ideas and topics in book:
* **Not-for-profit organisations** (see pg 9)
* **Corporate Structures** (see pg 75)
* **Social Enterprise** (see pg 74)
* **ICEDRIPS checklist** (see pg 28)
* **Mission** (see pg 11)
* **Vision** (see pg 11)
* **Values** (see pg 11)
* **Business Plan / Development Plan** (see pg 100)
* **Feasibility Filter** (see pg 90)

To conclude...

The objective of this book is to offer an approach which brings together both creative passion and business best practice.

T-Shirts and Suits – creativity and business in harmony.

1

Be clear about where you want to go and your own definition of success.

2

Select your customers carefully.
To turn your creativity into a business, use it for the benefit of your (carefully selected) customers. This involves understanding their point of view and then being even more creative with your talents.

3

Acknowledge the competition.
Decide where you stand amongst your rivals. Figure out which customers' problems you can solve better than anyone else.

4

Be a leader as well as a manager.
The art of getting things done through other people requires you to constantly strive to become an even better people person.

Protect your creativity – it's what your business is built on. Use copyright, trademarks and patents to protect your intellectual property. Exploit your intellectual property to create future income streams.

Measure the right things.
Design a simple but effective information system as a Business Dashboard so that you can keep a check on how you are performing in several dimensions as you drive your enterprise forward. Keep an eye on the Financial Dashboard to make sure you don't crash or run out of fuel in the fast lane.

Create a unique Business Formula.
A feasible Business Formula is essentially a carefully designed combination of some of your best creative skills, with selected customers' particular needs, which works in financial terms for them and you.

Use the Feasibility Filter to assess each option. Some creative business ideas may not be feasible. Be prepared to adjust an idea to get the Business Formula right. Or create new ideas.

Be prepared to Say No.
Once you have a clear route to success, 'say no' to tempting opportunities that don't lead towards your destination. Some temporary diversions will be necessary but don't lose sight of your goal.

Appendix 1
The Creative Industries

The 'creative industries' have been defined by the UK Government's Department for Culture, Media and Sport (DCMS)[28] as: 'Those industries which have their origin in individual creativity, skill and talent and which have a potential for wealth and job creation through the generation and exploitation of intellectual property.'

The term 'cultural industries' is also used by some agencies, though this term relates to a more specific range of industries and can be regarded as a subset of the creative industries. The cultural industries are defined by UNESCO[29] as 'industries that combine the creation, production and commercialisation of contents which are intangible and cultural in nature; these contents are typically protected by copyright and they can take the form of a good or a service.'

There are thirteen sub-sectors under the term 'creative industries' and these are: advertising; architecture; the art and antiques market; crafts; design; designer fashion; film and video; interactive leisure software; music; the performing arts; publishing; software and computer games; and television and radio.

According to DCMS[30] research, the Creative Industries accounted for 8.2% of Gross Value Added (GVA) in 2001 in the UK and the sector grew by an average of 8% per annum between 1997 and 2001. Exports from the UK by the Creative Industries contributed £11.4 billion to the balance of trade in 2001. This equated to around 4.2% of all goods and services exported. Exports for the Creative Industries grew at around 15% per annum over the period of 1997–2001. In June 2002, creative employment totalled 1.9 million jobs and there were around 122,000 companies in the Creative Industry sectors on the Inter-Departmental Business Register (IDBR) in 2002.

According to the *Financial Times*,[31] "a report from the (UK) Government's Strategy Unit has concluded that the creative industries in London are now more important than financial services to the economy. Employment in the creative industries (including fashion, software design, publishing, architecture and antique dealing) has topped 525,000 and is still rising, compared to a mere 322,000 and falling in financial services."

Internationally, the Creative Industries are one of the fastest growing sectors in OECD economies, employing on average 3–5% of the workforce according to the United Nations Conference on Trade and Development.[32] The global value of Creative Industries was expected to increase in the years from 2000 to 2005 from US$ 831 billion to US$ 1.3 trillion, a compound annual growth of over 7%.[33]

This astounding figure is achieved by creative businesses, most of which are small or medium sized enterprises and in reality are very small or micro-enterprises, including individual practitioners. The British Council[34] points out that this scenario is typical internationally and works to support international co-operation since creative businesses move more quickly to international markets than many other forms of enterprise, often using the Internet.

The Creative Industries are the only sector which has been identified as a priority area by all of the countries and regions of the UK. This is reflected by the number of agencies supporting the creative sector, such as CIDS (Creative Industries Development Service), CIDA (Creative Industries Development Agency), Inspiral and Creative Kernow.

The first of these to be established in the late 1990s was Merseyside ACME (Arts, Culture and Media Enterprises).

Appendix 2
Merseyside ACME

Merseyside ACME is a development agency for the Creative Industries sector, working to support the growth and sustainability of creative businesses and organisations based on Merseyside.

ACME works collaboratively with both the public and private sectors to:

- Promote the importance of the Creative Industries as an economic driver for the region.

- Ensure the availability and continuity of sector specific business support and information services.

- Promote the use of creativity as a means of supporting community and economic regeneration.

- Promote connectivity across the Creative Industries sector.

Complementing its strategic development role, ACME provides a range of general client-facing support services for creative businesses and organisations in the region. These include information and research support, and general business advice and referral services.

In addition to its ongoing general support services, ACME also delivers bespoke programmes, designed in direct response to feedback from the businesses that it works with.

As well as supporting creative businesses, ACME has developed projects which have shown how powerful and effective creativity can be in regenerating communities. It is respected nationally for its work on social impact studies,

for developing models and delivering programmes which promote best practice in monitoring and evaluation. It provides independent evaluation support services to community driven programmes and organisations across the UK.

Since being established, Merseyside ACME has:

- Worked with over 700 businesses and committed over £1.5m direct investment into the sector.

- Commissioned approximately £160,000 worth of research and generated over 300 jobs.

- Delivered over 70 industry seminars, reaching over 1500 creative professionals and practitioners.

- Has spearheaded the development of Kin, www.kin2kin.co.uk. Recognised as best practice in the field of collaboration and business engagement, this member driven initiative allows creative individuals, businesses and organisations in Liverpool and Merseyside to connect and promote themselves online, share ideas, contacts, news, advice and information.

- Developed a self-evaluation framework which has been adopted by organisations across the UK.

- Worked, through its arts and regeneration activity, with over 150 community regeneration projects, developed 30 new organisations and community businesses, invested more than £1m in community programmes and has published a significant social impact study, respected worldwide.

- Managed the Arts and Regeneration strand of Liverpool's bid to be European Capital of Culture 2008.

Merseyside
acme
DEVELOPING CREATIVE INDUSTRIES

kin linking Liverpool and Merseyside's creative people

References

1 Merseyside ACME (arts, culture, media, enterprise). *For more information see www.merseysideacme.com*
2 Creative Advantage. *For more information see www.creativeadvantage.co.uk or www.merseysideacme.com*
3 CIDS. Creative Industries Development Service. *For more information see www.cids.co.uk*
4 CIDA. Creative Industries Development Agency. *For more information see www.cida.org*
5 This is strictly true but modesty forbids me to let it go without a footnote. With one short poem published in a literary magazine, I claim to be the least-published 'published poet' in the world. On the other hand, having been paid five pounds for my Haiku of 17 syllables could make me one of the world's best-paid poets – per syllable (!)
6 Masters Degree in Business Administration (with distinction). Bradford University School of Management. 1995.
7 The 13 sub-sectors of the creative industries are: advertising; architecture; the art and antiques market; crafts; design; designer fashion; film and video; interactive leisure software; music; the performing arts; publishing; software and computer games; and television and radio.
8 Sun Tzu, *The Art of War*. Translation by Lionel Giles.
9 Interestingly, several words of military origin have been adapted for use in business, such as 'campaign' and 'strategy'.
10 Jim Collins, *Good to Great*. Random House. 2001.
11 When I used this concept on a consultancy project in the Middle East with a group of senior managers from different countries it became clear that many of them were not familiar with hedgehogs. I explained it is an animal with spikes on its back – a smaller version of the American porcupine.
12 *Guardian*. 08 November 2004.
13 W.Chan Kim and Renee Mauborgne, 'Charting Your Company's Future'. *Harvard Business Review*. 2002.
14 Michael Porter, *Competitive Strategy: Techniques for Analyzing Industries and Competitors*. Free Press. 1980.
15 Adam M. Brandenburger and Barry J. Nalebuff. *Co-opetition*. Harper Collins. 1996.
16 UK Government. Department for Culture Media and Sport (DCMS).
17 The Income and Expenditure Account can also be called a profit and loss account or income statement.
18 Handy, Charles, *The Age of Unreason*. Random House, London. 1989.
19 Pact is the UK trade association that represents and promotes the commercial interests of independent feature film, television, animation and interactive media companies. *See www.pact.co.uk*
20 Ofcom is the independent regulator and competition authority for the UK communications industries, with responsibilities across television, radio, telecommunications and wireless communications services. *See www.ofcom.org.uk*
21 Daniel Goleman, 'Leadership that gets results'. *Harvard Business Review*. March – April 2000.
22 Jim Collins, *Good to Great*. Random House. 2001.
23 *Inspirational Leadership*, UK Government, Department for Trade and Industry. 2004.
24 Readers wearing suits will recognise that this is inspired by the McKinsey/GE Matrix, which I have adapted for creative entrepreneurs wearing T-Shirts.
25 Bishop, Susan, 'The Strategic Power of Saying No'. *Harvard Business Review*. November – December. 1999.
26 *Guardian*. 08 November 2004.
27 Norton and Kaplan, 'The Balanced Scorecard: Translating Strategy into Action'. *Harvard Business Review*. 1996.
28 Mapping Document, Creative Industries Unit and Taskforce. UK Government Department for Culture, Media and Sport (DCMS). October 1998.
29 UNESCO, Paris. 2000. Culture, Trade and Globalisation: Questions and Answers.
30 UK Government Department for Culture, Media and Sport (DCMS).
31 *Financial Times*. 04 July 2003.
32 UNCTAD, Geneva. 2004. Creative Industries and Development.
33 Howkins, John, *The Creative Economy: How People Make Money from Ideas*. Allen Lane, London. 2001.
34 British Council. *www.britishcouncil.org*

Index

Author's Acknowledgements

I would like to thank all at Merseyside ACME and all those who have helped me in their various ways to make this book possible, especially Phil Birchenall, Helen Bowyer, Helen Brazier, Peter Burke, Jonathan Butters, Anthony Byrne, Mike Carney, Marc Collett, Gemma Coupe, Andrew Critchley, Richard Engelhardt, Matt Finnegan, Noel Fitzsimmons, Kate Fletcher, David Gettman, Julian Grice, Geoffrey Horley, David Hughes, Ian Hughes, Matt Johnson, Marc Jones, Moira Kenny, Andy Lovatt, Aitor Mate, Kevin McManus, Chris Morris, Sharon Mutch, Bridgette O'Connor, Kath Oversby, Andrew Patrick, Ecaterina Petreanu, Cathy Skelly, Jane Thomas, Marius Ursache, Richard Veal, Dave Ward, Geoff White and Pete Wylie.

Further Information

The website associated with this book provides additional information, new material and further case studies, details of training and consultancy projects, a framework for a business plan, a glossary of terms and links to other useful websites.

www.t-shirtsandsuits.com

Merseyside
acme
DEVELOPING CREATIVE INDUSTRIES

T-Shirts and Suits®

Publisher's Acknowledgements

Merseyside ACME wishes to thank all those organisations and individuals who have collaborated with this project including the supply of images and the permission for their use.